NUCLEAR PHYSICS IN PEACE
AND WAR

IS VOLUME

128

OF THE

Twentieth Century Encyclopedia of Catholicism

UNDER SECTION

XIII

CATHOLICISM AND SCIENCE

IT IS ALSO THE

67TH

VOLUME IN ORDER OF PUBLICATION

THE TWENTIETH CENTURY ENCYCLOPEDIA · OF CATHOLICISM ·

Edited by HENRI DANIEL-ROPS of the Académie Française

NUCLEAR PHYSICS
IN PEACE AND WAR

By PETER E. HODGSON

HAWTHORN BOOKS · PUBLISHERS · *New York*

First Edition, June, 1961

NIHIL OBSTAT

Andreas Moore, L.C.L.

Censor Deputatus

IMPRIMATUR

E. Morrogh Bernard

Vicarius Generalis

Westmonasterii, die II MAII MCMLXI

The Nihil obstat and Imprimatur are a declaration that a book or pamphlet is considered to be free from doctrinal or moral error. It is not implied that those who have granted the Nihil obstat and Imprimatur agree with the contents, opinions or statements expressed.

CONTENTS

ABBREVIATIONS

Reference is frequently made to articles in the following periodicals:

BAS *Bulletin of the Atomic Scientists* (published by the Educational Foundation for Nuclear Science, Inc., Chicago, Illinois, U.S.A.).

ASN *Atomic Scientists' News*, later *Atomic Scientists' Journal*
ASJ (published for the Atomic Scientists' Association of Great Britain by Messrs. Taylor and Francis, Ltd., London).

NS The *New Scientist* (London).

APD *Atoms for Peace Digest* (published by the United States Information Service, London, W.1).

INTRODUCTION

The theme of this book is the discoveries made in this century about the nucleus of the atom, and the effects of these discoveries on the lives of men. From the efforts of a few people, working alone and unheeded in small laboratories, there has sprung in a very few years a river of change and innovation, of fresh insights and new powers, that is still in full spate. It has flowed over the boundaries of nuclear physics into the other sciences: astronomy, chemistry, biology, engineering have alike received powerful stimulus from it. Ranging still further afield, it has put new tools into the hands of the geologist, the archaeologist, the agriculturalist and the industrialist. It has lent new strength to the healing hands of the doctor and the surgeon, and to the defending, the destroying, the oppressing hands of the men of war. It has created problems to tax the ingenuity of lawyers and agonize the consciences of the moralists. In all these ways, and in countless others, it is flowing into the lives of every man and woman on this earth. It is a river that flows into the valley of peace or into the abyss of war.

Yet who is at all qualified to speak of these changes? Though they have taken place within the lifetimes of most of us, they are already so extensive and far-reaching as to exceed the understanding of any man. A panel of experts would be needed to give even a brief outline of all that has been done, and then they would write not a simple book for the average man, but a shelf of treatises that few would read and none absorb to the full.

It is possible that a more modest attempt may be of some use. Since no one can claim expert knowledge of all the aspects of the effects of nuclear physics, it might be interest-

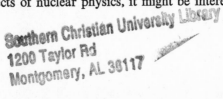

ing to present them as seen through the eyes of one scientist, who has watched the results of the work of his predecessors, and tried to understand a little of what is happening.

Whether one thinks that such an attempt is at all useful depends on one's conception of the place of the scientist in human society. Should he get on with his own job and keep his mouth shut, or should he from his pinnacle of knowledge lay down the rules of the society of the future? These two extreme views are worth probing a little more, as by contrast they can lead to a more balanced view of the proper place of the scientist. They are the twin poles of a curiously ambivalent attitude towards the scientist. The scientist, people feel, has access to hidden knowledge, and can bring about events that would be incredible if we did not see them happening before our eyes. Is he the wise man to whom we should entrust our future, or the menace who should be locked up?

The pursuit of science requires long and arduous study that appears to leave little time for anything else. Hence it seems that the knowledge of the scientist has been bought at a fearful price; not only is he unlikely to have anything useful to say on everyday human affairs, but his judgement is likely to be positively warped by his single-mindedness of purpose. He is a specialist and is there to answer specialized questions. Let him get on with his work; but when we want to know how to get over a technical difficulty we can ask him to produce the right gadgets for us.

So thought some early industrialists. The scientist was just a superior sort of workman who had mastered a certain skill. He was summoned to the boardroom, expected to answer a complex question with a yes or a no, and then dismissed. Some scientists put up with this treatment, and contributed virtually nothing to the industry they served. Others refused to see their work wasted, and more forward-looking boards made a place for them among their number. They soon found that the scientist, who perhaps was not very illuminating when asked to answer their questions, was much better at telling them what questions they ought to have been asking him. Instead of helping to solve problems arising in the course of long-traditional work, the scientists were able to open up whole new areas of activity. New processes, new products poured from their fertile minds. They alone could see in some obscure research the seeds of a vast new industry, or point to the coming decay of one established from time immemorial. The chemical industry was the first to reap the fruits of the insight of the scientist, and others soon followed. The view that the scientist should be "on tap, but not on top", was heard no more, and his place was established in the councils of industry.

A rather similar story could be told of the scientist and the soldier. Military men understand war, and know what they require to fight it more effectively. They want a gun that shoots farther or a tank that moves faster. They brief the scientist, he sets to work, and the required improvement is made. But the more imaginative scientist is not satisfied with this, and applies the method of science to war itself. He thinks not of what the military ask him to do, but of what they ought to be asking him to do. Instead of an improvement he produces a revolution. Instead of better signalling with flags and smoke, he produces wireless. Instead of better telescopes, he produces radar. And instead of better T.N.T., he produces the atomic bomb. Like the industrialists, the military have discovered that the scientist cannot be treated as simply a useful assistant; he must share their inner councils if he is to realize his potential to the full.

Gratified by his success, the scientist may come to see himself as possessor of the universal method of solving all problems. He is the one with the knowledge to direct the future course of civilization. Only he has the insight and the knowledge to steer the evolution of man.

And yet when he tries to do so the result is all too often rather disappointing. It is frequently manifest that he has not at all grasped the subtleties of the difficulties he so glibly settles. He discourses on politics, on law, on philosophy and on religion with a naïvety that astonishes not only the expert, but even those with a very little knowledge of these fields. Then there arises a demand that he stick to what he knows about and leave other people's subjects alone. So the wheel comes the full circle and he is pushed back into the specialized world from which he has so recently emerged.

Scientists are not the only ones who, with the best of intentions, make fools of themselves. It frequently happens that statesmen, military men, lawyers and churchmen, to say nothing of politicians and journalists, will, with all the weight of their undoubted authority, pronounce on some question of the day completely oblivious to some simple fact that entirely vitiates their conclusions. The expert will not be popular when he points this out, but if he does not do so, who will? Yet how is he to do this constructively, without seeming either maliciously to puncture the omniscience of the distinguished or without falling into the same trap himself when he ventures outside his own field?

A way out of this impasse can be found by looking at how the scientist solves the problems of cooperation and integration of two techniques in his own field. The complexity of modern science is such that frequently many scientists are needed to attack a single problem. Each is familiar with only one or two of the many techniques that he and his colleagues have to apply. Perhaps one part of the work could be done very easily, but only at the cost of putting intolerable difficulties and complications on another part. It can be a matter of the greatest delicacy to decide exactly how to bring about the harmonious union of the different techniques so as to achieve the desired result with the least overall effort.

No one man knows enough to think it all out and apportion the work himself. A satisfactory solution can only come through full, free and frank discussion extending over many months. No one stands on ceremony about putting his own wishes to the fore, or is surprised when they are subjected to the most thorough and relentless criticism. Half-formed, even superficially absurd ideas are thrown into the pool, and often a more useful one arises from the very process of their refutation. No one thinks any the less of his colleagues for suggesting such ideas; a start has to be made somewhere when all are groping in the dark. No one is upset at his ideas being torn to shreds, for that is the only way to truth. Each must be sufficiently attached to his ideas to lavish care on developing and strengthening them, and on defending them against attack, and yet be neither surprised nor disappointed when searching analysis reduces them to ashes. Between the scientists there is what physicists call a high coupling constant; each person acts and reacts strongly on the others, and the whole group is welded into one by the strength of the interaction, and is enabled to achieve what would be quite beyond the powers of the individual members of the group. The slightest trace of dogmatism or intolerance, or lack of willingness to meet the others more than half-way, of bad temper or inflexibility, is sufficient to cripple the process or even to kill it stone dead.

The main trouble about the relations between the scientist and the statesman, the lawyer and the rest, is that frequently the coupling constant between them is extremely small. There is nothing like the necessary discussion and interchange of views on the problem concerned before a pronouncement is made or a disastrous course of action decided upon. Then it is too late for the scientist to do more than complain or laugh, and this makes it even less likely that he will ever be consulted again.

This will indicate something of the spirit in which this book is written. I do not want to appear to lay down the law on a number of subjects that I quite manifestly know very little about. I simply want to describe how things look to me and, where necessary, to "stick my neck out" on controversial questions whose solution, in so far as there is one, can only come from a discussion like that described above between those familiar with all the problems involved. If it serves only to indicate some of the problems to be solved, and to stimulate further thought on them, it will be worth while.

A word should be said on the place of the present book in this series. A consideration of the Church in the twentieth century cannot be complete unless it takes account of contemporary scientific developments, for these affect both the ideas and the material conditions of man's life. The Church does not exist in a vacuum, but in a world that is being increasingly moulded by science. The main purpose of this book is to show how nuclear physics is influencing the world today. It is mainly factual, and provides some of the background to many of the other books in the series.

In so small a compass as this, completeness cannot be attempted, so frequent references are made to other published works to enable any particular topic to be followed up in more detail. These references are themselves incomplete, being simply a few of the sources that have come to my notice.

The more controversial questions concerning the applications of nuclear physics receive only brief mention, more to indicate what needs to be discussed than to provide final answers. Many of the views expressed here will not be shared by other Catholics, and beyond the justification they carry intrinsically, I would claim no more than that they may be held by a Catholic.

I cannot end this introduction without thanking those with whom I have discussed many of the matters touched upon here. Among them are my colleagues of the Atomic Scientists' Association with whom I have worked for many years to bring about a greater understanding of the human problems raised by nuclear physics. Foremost among these is Professor J. Rotblat, whose tireless enthusiasm is an inspiration to all who have the pleasure of working with him. My gratitude goes also to my friends in university and parliamentary life, who have to some extent succeeded in opening my eyes to the complexities of the affairs of men. At the head of these is the Rt. Hon. P. J. Noel-Baker, P.C., M.P., with whom I had the privilege of numerous discussions while he was writing his book on disarmament and the international control of atomic energy.

CHAPTER I

BASIC NUCLEAR PHYSICS

On the shield of the United Kingdom Atomic Energy Authority there is the motto *E minimis maxima*, from the smallest causes come the greatest effects. This is indeed one of the most remarkable features of the story of the atomic nuclei and their effects on mankind. The nucleus is so small that a million million of them, placed side by side, would barely span one of the full stops on this page. Yet it has been discovered and probed and analysed by the restless curiosity of scientists, it has yielded many of its secrets to patient and daring experimentation, and has finally been harnessed to the purposes of man. Each nucleus can give only a little energy, yet millions of millions of them, all adding their share, can combine together to give the spectacular results with which we are all so familiar.

EARLY HISTORY OF ATOMIC ENERGY

If the motto is true physically, it is also true in human terms. The whole atomic industry, now employing millions of people throughout the world, sprang from the work of a handful of men in the Cavendish Laboratory of the University of Cambridge and a very few other laboratories in the first few decades of the present century. The roots of this work go back far into the past, from the speculations of Democritus through Scaliger's work in the Middle Ages to Dalton, Avogadro, Becquerel and Curie.[1] Towards the end of the

[1] *From Atomos to Atom. The History of the Concept Atom*, A. G. van Melsen, Duquesne Univ. Press, Pittsburgh, 1952.

nineteenth century, J. J. Thomson[2] had gathered around him an enthusiastic group of young men and together they discovered the electron and laid the foundations of our knowledge of electronic and ionic phenomena, and the structure of the atom.

He was succeeded in 1919 by Rutherford,[3] who discovered the nucleus of the atom and led the way in the elucidation of nuclear structure. Many of those who worked with him have become well known beyond the borders of physics—Sir John Cockcroft, the first to split the atom, later Director of the Atomic Energy Research Establishment at Harwell and now Master of Churchill College, Cambridge; Sir George Thomson, who discovered the wave nature of the electron; Sir James Chadwick who discovered the neutron; Sir Charles Darwin (grandson of the biologist) and Professors N. F. Mott and Sir Harrie Massey, pioneers of wave mechanics, and a score of others.

These early researches were almost unknown to the public a decade before they made their dramatic impact on world affairs. They received negligible financial support. For example, the total expenditure on equipment for forty research workers at the Cavendish Laboratory for the year 1912–13 was in the region of £500 (or, in those days, about $2,000).[4] For the most part they had to make their apparatus, their electrometers and vacuum pumps, with their own hands. They had no idea of what their researches would lead to. Their motivation was that of scientists everywhere, to find out more about the world in which we live. This is the driving curiosity that leads us to devote our lives to the study of minute and apparently insignificant effects which may yet be another clue to the ultimate structure of matter. Naturally, scientists are gratified when their work finds some beneficial application, but that is not the prime motive. It is usually

[2] J. J. Thomson, *Recollections and Reflections*, Bell, London, 1936.
[3] A. S. Eve, *Rutherford*, Cambridge Univ. Press, 1939.
[4] J. J. Thomson, *loc. cit.*, p. 126.

impossible to foresee the practical results of any particular research in pure science. It is a venture into the unknown, and this is what gives it its attraction and excitement. This is true of all research in pure science, but seldom is it more spectacularly illustrated than by nuclear research. Even Rutherford himself, asked in 1933 whether he thought there would be any useful results of his work, said he thought the energy of the nucleus would never be released on a large scale, and he held to this view until his death in 1936.[5] Yet only two years later nuclear fission was discovered and the race for the atomic bomb began.

ATOMIC AND NUCLEAR STRUCTURE

It is fortunate that it is possible to understand these developments on the basis of quite simple conceptions of the structure of atoms and their interactions with each other. We can picture nuclei as tiny billiard balls and gain a real insight into their behaviour. Providing we are willing to accept a number of facts without wanting to know the reasons behind them, these simple pictures are all that is needed to understand the essentials of nuclear physics and its applications.

The billiard-ball picture is, of course, only a part of the story. It gives a good approximation to the behaviour of particles that are moving very rapidly, as is usually the case for the effects that interest us here. But when they move more slowly, other effects become prominent that can only be understood by supposing that the "particles" have a wave aspect as well. Here pictorial language and our everyday imagination begin to break down and we have to use the abstract mathematical conceptions of quantum mechanics. To understand the behaviour of nuclei in detail quite subtle physics and complicated mathematics is needed. Nuclear

[5] C. P. Snow, *The Two Cultures and the Scientific Revolution*, Cambridge University Press, 1959, p. 31; Sir George Thomson, *ASN*, **2**, 345 (1953).

physics has developed so extensively over the last twenty years that it is usual to spend one's life studying just one small part of it. But luckily we do not have to know it all before we are able to understand its applications.

Using the simple picture, we can imagine a typical atom as composed of a small, hard central core, called the nucleus, surrounded by a cloud of lighter particles called electrons. It is not unlike the solar system, with the planets surrounding the central sun. The electron cloud forms the surface of the atom and is the only part that participates in the relatively gentle chemical changes such as those that occur in cooking, burning and even in the explosion of T.N.T. This was the part of the atom that was studied around the turn of the century by J. J. Thomson and his colleagues.

Throughout all these chemical changes the core of the atom, the nucleus, remains unchanged. Here resides most of the mass of the atom, and the charge on the nucleus determines whether the atom shall be hydrogen, oxygen, iron, sulphur or any one of the 100 or so different chemical elements. The number of electrons circling the nucleus is also proportional to the nuclear charge, so a light atom like carbon has six electrons, while a heavy one like uranium has ninety-two.

In 1919 Aston, a colleague of Rutherford in Cambridge, devised a way of measuring the masses of individual nuclei. Charged particles are deflected when they are sent through electric and magnetic fields, and the higher their charge and the smaller their mass the greater the deflection. So he shot beams of nuclei through electric and magnetic fields, and found that particles of different charge and mass were sent in different directions. He discovered that nuclei of the same element, and therefore having the same nuclear charge, could often occur with several different masses. Argon, for example, having average nuclear weight of 21, is a mixture of nuclei of masses 20 and 22. Hydrogen is a mixture of nuclei of masses 1, 2 and 3, called respectively protons, deuterons and tritons.

These nuclei of the same charge but different mass are called isotopes of the element concerned. Many of the elements occurring naturally are mixtures of several isotopes, and many new isotopes not found naturally have since been made synthetically.

The neutron and nuclear structure

These facts about the different types of nuclei were explained by Chadwick's discovery of the neutron in 1932. This is a neutral particle having nearly the same mass as a proton, the lightest nucleus. All nuclei are composed of neutrons and protons, and they are held together by the nuclear forces. The number of protons, each carrying unit positive charge, gives the charge of the nucleus, and hence the chemical element. The electrons going round the nucleus each have one unit negative charge as well, and there is one for each nuclear proton, so that the atom as a whole is neutral. The mass of the nucleus is proportional to the sum of the number of protons and the number of neutrons.

In most nuclei there are about the same numbers of neutrons as protons, though in the heavier nuclei there tends to be an excess of neutrons. For example, the isotopes of hydrogen are the proton, a proton and one neutron, and a proton and two neutrons respectively. Those of a medium weight element like ordinary copper have 29 protons and 34 or 36 neutrons, and those of a heavy element like uranium have 92 protons and 143 or 146 neutrons. These isotopes of the same elements behave in the same way chemically, but they often have very different nuclear properties. It is thus necessary, when considering a particular type of nucleus, to specify both the number of protons and the number of neutrons it contains.

Atoms of different elements can combine together to form molecules like water, composed of hydrogen and oxygen, and

common salt, composed of sodium and chlorine. Some molecules, like those in living bodies, are exceedingly complex
structures composed of many thousands of atoms delicately
arranged in particular patterns. All matter is ultimately
composed of atoms and molecules built up from nuclei and
electrons. The nucleus, itself remaining unchanged, thus
governs the behaviour of the atom and hence of all material
things.

Radioactive transformations

In exceptional circumstances the nucleus itself can change.
A few types of nuclei, like radium, are inherently unstable or
radioactive. After a lapse of time that may be only a small
fraction of a second or may be millions of years they spon-
taneously shoot out a particle or a pulse of high-frequency
radiation.

The time of breakup or decay of a particular radioactive
nucleus cannot be predicted or influenced in any way, but
observations on a large number of decays shows that the
probability of decay remains constant with time. It is just as
likely to break up in one minute as in the next. (This may be
compared with men, who are more likely to die as time goes
on, and with radio valves, that are less likely to fail the longer
they keep on working.) Expressed mathematically, the radioactivity, or number of radioactive nuclei in a given mass of
radioactive material, decays exponentially with time. The
rate of decay depends on the type of nucleus, and is described
by the half-life, which is the time that elapses before half the
nuclei in a given mass of radioactive material have decayed.
Thus, for example, if the half-life of a radioactive nucleus is
one week, half of them will be intact after one week, a
quarter after two weeks, an eighth after three weeks and so
on. In each succeeding week the radioactivity is reduced to
a half of its value at the beginning of that week.

When it undergoes radioactive decay, a nucleus can emit
either an alpha particle or an electron or a gamma ray. An

alpha particle is simply a nucleus of helium, consisting of two protons and two neutrons, while a gamma ray is a pulse of high-frequency electromagnetic radiation.

Ionization

After it has been emitted from the radioactive nucleus, the alpha particle, electron or gamma ray tears through any matter it encounters, frequently knocking electrons out of atoms in its path. This leaves the atoms positively charged, as they lack one or more electrons. These charged atoms are known as ions, and the knocking-out process is called ionization. The alpha particles and electrons, being charged, can act on the electrons by their electric fields, and so can knock out electrons from atoms some distance away from their path. They therefore ionize continually and a dense trail of ions is left in their wake. By techniques like the cloud chamber and the nuclear emulsion this trail of ions can be made visible, showing exactly where the particle has gone.

For particles of the same velocity, the ionization is proportional to the square of the charge. The alpha particles thus ionize much more heavily than electrons. Since ionization absorbs energy, they are more rapidly brought to rest. This has important biological implications.

Gamma rays are uncharged, and can only knock out electrons by occasional direct impacts. They do not therefore leave a dense trail of ions, but just a few here and there. Most of the gamma-ray ionization is due to the fast ejected electrons. The gamma rays are thus more penetrating than the charged particles. In a similar way neutrons, which are sometimes formed in fast beams, do not ionize continually, but produce considerable indirect ionization by the protons they eject from atoms and nuclei.

All these effects of fast nuclear particles can be used to detect their presence. The visual techniques showing the path of the particle have already been mentioned. Another instrument, the Geiger-Müller counter, amplifies the ionization electronically and records an electric pulse whenever a charged nuclear particle passes through it.

NUCLEAR REACTIONS

After a radioactive nucleus has emitted one particle it may still be radioactive and liable to emit another particle or a gamma ray, or it may be stable. Even stable nuclei, however, can be broken up by very energetic collisions with other nuclei. Thus, if hydrogen nuclei, that is, protons, are accelerated to high energies by electric fields of hundreds of thousands of volts, they can collide violently with other nuclei and break them up. This is called a nuclear reaction. Alternatively, two colliding nuclei may coalesce to form a larger nucleus. Nuclear physics is essentially the study of these changes and what they can tell us about the structure of nuclei.[6]

Nuclear energy

It had long been suspected that vast stores of energy are locked inside the nucleus. Einstein in his theory of relativity had given reasons for supposing that mass and energy were in a sense equivalent and that if mass M were converted into energy, the amount of energy formed would be $E=MC^2$, where C is the velocity of light. If this is worked out numerically, it becomes clear that a very small mass is equivalent to an immense amount of energy.[7]

When Cockcroft and Walton split the atom, they found that the masses of the products were slightly less than that of the colliding nuclei, and when this mass deficit was converted into energy by Einstein's equation it agreed accurately with

[6] For fuller accounts of the structure of the atom see, *Inside the Atom*, by I. Asimov, Abelard Schuman 1956; *Finding Out about Atomic Energy*, by J. L. Michiels, Thrift Books No. 6, 1951; *Atomic Energy*, Ed. by J. L. Crammer and R. E. Peierls, Pelican No. A224, 1950.

[7] The fission of 1 kg of uranium releases 22,700,000 kWh. H. Thirring, "The Super Bomb", *BAS*, 6, 69 (1950). This is equivalent to the explosion of 20,000 tons of TNT, or the burning of 1,400 tons of coal

the observed energy release of the reaction. The snag was that a lot of energy had to be expended to accelerate the colliding nuclei before the reaction could begin, and only about one in a million of the accelerated particles actually initiated a reaction. So, although there was an energy gain in each individual reaction, the process as a whole required a net expenditure of energy. The theory of the transformation of mass into energy was thus confirmed, but there seemed no way of realizing it economically.

Thermonuclear reactions

Another approach, also of extreme simplicity, was similarly baulked by practical difficulties. The idea was to use the natural thermal motion of atoms, and therefore of the nuclei they contain, to initiate the reaction. In any gas the mole-cules are flying around with considerable energy, continually bouncing off each other and the walls of the vessel containing them. This is why a gas exerts a pressure. As the temperature of the gas is increased, so is the velocity of the gas molecules and hence the pressure of the gas. If the volume is kept the same, the pressure is proportional to the absolute temperature. If the gas is composed of nuclei such as those of some types of hydrogen that are known to react together with the pro-duction of energy, all that has to be done is to increase the temperature until the nuclear reaction begins. Once this happens, the heat generated will suffice to keep the gas hot enough for the reaction to continue.

This proposal avoids the difficulty of the previous approach, since each hydrogen nucleus goes on making collisions in-definitely, while before it only had a small chance of making one. So even if the chance of reacting during a collision is very small, it will ultimately happen.

The principle of this method of obtaining energy from the atom is sound, but it is defeated by a practical detail: if we work out the temperature the gas has to be before the reaction can start it comes out in the region of 10 million degrees. This is far beyond the highest temperatures, about 5,000 degrees, that can be reached by ordinary chemical means. Even if we could attain it, the vessel containing the gas would instantly vaporize.

Though this difficulty seems insurmountable, it has proved possible, as will be seen later, to ignite the gas by another type of nuclear reaction. Once the reaction begins it proceeds with explosive violence, and is in fact the hydrogen bomb. Reactions like these, that proceed by the heating-up of the whole mass of the reacting substances, are called thermo-nuclear reactions. It is from reactions of this type that stars derive their energy, and they are only prevented from ex-ploding by certain automatic control mechanisms. Occasion-ally these fail, and then we have the phenomena of the novae and supernovae, stars that suddenly increase in brilliance and then gradually fade into insignificance.

This was the position in the late 'thirties on the problem of tapping the stores of energy known to reside in the nuclei of atoms. The idea was sound in principle, the theory had been verified, but no practical way could be found to realize it.

Nuclear fission

The whole situation was altered by the discovery of nuclear fission towards the end of 1938. This is an unusual and curious effect which in a sense need never have occurred. It would be quite easy to imagine the whole of nuclear physics remaining the same without nuclear fission. It is so outside the main stream that it is possible to study nuclear physics for years without needing to know anything at all about fission. And yet it proved to be the long-sought key to releasing the energy in the nucleus.

Fission was discovered in the course of a systematic series of researches into the properties of the heavy nuclei. Efforts were being made to make a series of elements heavier than uranium, the heaviest that occurs naturally. This was done by bombarding uranium with neutrons. As these are neutral, they can enter and stick to a nucleus with much less difficulty than charged particles. Sure enough, an apparently new element was found in minute quantities after the irradiation. It was analysed by chemists in Germany and, to their astonishment, turned out to be, not the expected transuranic element, but barium, an element whose nucleus is roughly half the size of the uranium nucleus. Professor O. Frisch and Dr L. Meitner realized the only possible explanation: the uranium nucleus must have been made unstable by the capture of a neutron so that it broke up into two roughly equal pieces.

The chain reaction

This was very interesting and curious, but not of any practical use. It became really exciting when it was found that as it split into two the uranium nucleus also emitted two or three more neutrons. These neutrons could themselves enter nearby uranium nuclei to cause more fissions, and yet more neutrons would be emitted and so on. This is a nuclear chain reaction. Even if only two of the neutrons from each fission cause another fission, in about twenty "generations" over a million uranium nuclei will have undergone fission. The time taken by a neutron to travel from one uranium nucleus to the next is exceedingly small, less than a millionth of a second, so it is not long from the entry of the first neutron to the fission of most of the uranium nuclei present.

The split halves of the uranium nuclei, or fission fragments as they are called, fly apart with great energy. They are gradually brought to rest by collisions with other nuclei and in the process impart energy to them. They are also highly radioactive and when they decay the particles they emit give more energy to their surroundings. Thus the energy released in the fission process appears ultimately as thermal energy, or heat, of the uranium. So as fissions occur in a block of uranium it rapidly gets warmer. Heat energy has been obtained from the nucleus. The process is a cheap one, because one neutron can cause an unlimited number of fissions through the chain reaction. This initial neutron need not cost anything, because there are always a few free neutrons around, liberated by the action of the cosmic rays on the nuclei in the air.

In practice, a number of conditions must be satisfied before the chain reaction can proceed. There must be more than a certain critical amount of uranium present. If there is insufficient, so many of the neutrons will leave the uranium or be absorbed by impurities in it that there are not enough remaining to keep the reaction going. Since the number of neutrons produced is proportional to the volume of the uranium, while the number escaping is proportional to its surface area, the more uranium there is the greater the proportion of the neutrons that do not escape and so are available to carry on the reaction. The uranium must be exceedingly pure if the impurities in it are not to absorb too many of the neutrons. This raises difficult chemical and metallurgical problems.

A further difficulty is due to the fact that natural uranium is a mixture of two different types or isotopes of uranium nuclei, called U235 and U238. Both isotopes have the same nuclear charge of 92, but they differ slightly in mass. If three neutrons could be added simultaneously to U235, the result would be U238. Of these two types of uranium nuclei, only U235 will undergo fission with slow neutrons, and it only occurs to the extent of one part in 140, or about seven-tenths of one per cent, of natural uranium. U238 also absorbs slow neutrons, thus removing them from the chain reaction, but it does not undergo fission. Instead it changes, by the successive emission of two electrons, into neptunium and then into plutonium, which itself can undergo fission.

There are thus two ways of obtaining pure fissile material: either by separating the U235 from the mixture of U235 and U238 that constitutes natural uranium, or by using the chain reaction in natural uranium to convert U238 into the fissile plutonium. Both ways, so simple in conception, lead to formidable technical difficulties when they are put into practice.

Separation of uranium isotopes

The chief difficulty in separating U235 from U238 is that they are identical chemically; there is no chemical method of separating the two types of uranium. Usually, when we want to separate two metals, it is sufficient to find an acid that will dissolve one and not the other, and the separation is achieved at once. But the two types of uranium, having the same nuclear charge, have almost exactly the same chemical properties, and so no method of separation along these lines is possible.

The method, if it is to succeed, has to be a physical one that depends on the difference in mass between the two types of uranium. A number of ways of doing this can be imagined, and of these two proved practicable on a large scale. They are the gaseous diffusion and the electromagnetic separation methods.

The first of these makes use of the fact that if a gas diffuses through a porous barrier, like a thin, unglazed earthenware jar, for example, the rate of diffusion depends on the density of the gas. Light gases get through faster than heavy ones, which is just what we would expect. So now if we can somehow make our natural uranium into a gas and pass it through a porous barrier it will emerge slightly enriched in U235, and what is left behind will be correspondingly depleted. If this is repeated again and again, we can ultimately obtain U235 to any desired degree of purity.

Again, there are difficulties when the details are worked out. It is not easy to make uranium, one of the heaviest of metals, into a gas. The only practicable gas is uranium hexafluoride, a compound of one atom of uranium with six of fluorine. It is not a pleasant substance to handle. It readily decomposes, thus blocking the pores of the diffusion barrier and releasing fluorine, one of the most poisonous and corrosive gases known to man. The difference in mass between the molecules of gas containing the two types of uranium is less than one per cent, so the degree of enrichment at each passage through the barrier is exceedingly small. These difficulties, however, were successfully overcome, and enough U235 was obtained in this way for the bomb that was dropped on Hiroshima. It is now the established method for extracting U235 from natural uranium.

The second method employs what is essentially a scaled-up mass spectrometer like the one used by Aston to discover isotopes. This depends on the principle that if a nucleus of an atom passes through a magnetic field its direction of motion is changed. It follows a curved path through the field, and the curvature depends on the mass and the charge of the nucleus concerned. For nuclei of the same charge, the curvature depends on the mass; the lighter nuclei are deflected more than the heavier ones. This is similar to driving a car round a bend; the heavier the car, the more force is needed to make it follow the curve. If, then, a mixture of U235 and U238 nuclei are shot between the poles of a powerful electromagnet, the beam will separate into two, the U235 being more strongly deflected than the U238. This is a slow process, as there is a limit to the amount of uranium that can be in flight at any one time. But here again the difficulties were solved, and substantial amounts of U235 were separated during the war by this method. It has now been superseded by the gaseous diffusion process.

NUCLEAR REACTORS

Plutonium

The other way of making fissile material from natural uranium is by converting the plentiful U238 into the fissile plutonium. To do this a chain reaction must be started in natural uranium. This requires rather a delicate balance between the proportion of neutrons needed to keep the chain reaction going, and the proportion used to convert the U238 into plutonium. The neutrons lost by escaping from the uranium or by capture by impurities in it must be reduced to the minimum. This is done by having a large amount of uranium, tens or hundreds of tons of it, and insisting that the uranium is of the highest purity. Even then, it is found that rather too many of the neutrons are captured by the U238, so that there are not enough to keep the chain reaction going. On investigation, it turns out that it is the fast neutrons, emitted direct from the fission process, that are most likely to be captured by the U238, while the slow ones are more likely to go into the U235, producing further fissions. So what is wanted is a way of slowing some of the neutrons down before they have a chance of being captured by the U238. This is done by interleaving the bars of uranium with a substance called a moderator. The complete pile, as it is called, thus consists of uranium and moderator, and it is possible to combine them so as to produce substantial amounts of plutonium, while leaving enough neutrons to keep the chain reaction going. A pile is also frequently referred to as a nuclear reactor.

Several materials can be used as a moderator. The main requirements are that it should be light, because light nuclei are more efficient in slowing down neutrons than heavy ones. It should not absorb the neutrons, for this would defeat its purpose, and it should be cheap and easy to handle. Of the light nuclei, most are excluded by one or other of these conditions with the exception of heavy water, which is very efficient but rather expensive, and carbon, which is not so efficient but very cheap. The first piles, and most of the large power reactors, therefore, used carbon in the form of graphite blocks. There are also a number of research reactors that use heavy water.

Control of nuclear reactors

Once the chain reaction is established in a reactor it will continue to build up until it explodes. It must, therefore, be carefully controlled so that the reaction proceeds steadily without reaching the explosion point. This is done by inserting control rods containing material that very readily absorbs neutrons, such as boron or cadmium. When, therefore, the chain reaction has reached a sufficient level, the control rods are pushed in until the multiplication factor is reduced to unity, that is, as many neutrons are produced in every generation as are absorbed. The reaction then proceeds steadily until so much uranium has been consumed by the fission process that increasing numbers of neutrons are being absorbed by the fission fragments, thus reducing the multiplication factor below one. This can be restored by pulling out the control rods slightly, but ultimately there comes a time when the reactor is so clogged by the "ash" of the fission fragments that the chain reaction can no longer proceed.

All the time the chain reaction is going, U238 is being changed into plutonium, and also heat is being produced. In the early reactors the plutonium was the main objective, and so the heat was allowed to run to waste. In the power reactors, however, as will be seen later, this heat is used to generate electricity.

After the reaction has died down, the uranium rods contain small amounts of plutonium and also of the fission fragments. These can all be separated from each other chemically. The plutonium is purified for use in bombs or other reactors, the uranium is made into new rods to be used again, and the fission fragments are kept for the many industrial applications that have been found for them.

There is no difficulty in principle about this separation, but it all has to be done by remote control because the fission products and the plutonium are highly radioactive and it would be dangerous for anyone to go too near them. Complex automatic processes have now been developed, so it can all be done behind concrete shielding without endangering the operators.

In practice, it is not necessary to shut down the reactor to extract the plutonium. The rods of uranium lie in long channels passing through the matrix of graphite blocks, and as new rods are inserted at one end of the channels, the used rods drop out at the other into a cooling pond where, shielded by water, their high radioactivity decays to a manageable level. The rods are then stripped of their protective case and dissolved in a waiting bath of acid to begin the first stage of the separation process.

These basic processes for the extraction of fissile material from natural uranium were developed in great secrecy during the war, and eventually made the atomic bomb possible. After the war, the same physics was applied for peaceful purposes and nuclear reactors were designed primarily to produce heat for the generation of electric power. These applications form the subject of the next three chapters, and show how the same physical processes can be applied in war and in peace.

CHAPTER II

NUCLEAR SCIENCE
AT WAR

Fission was discovered in Berlin by Hahn and Strassmann towards the end of 1938. It is interesting to reflect on what might have happened had Hitler realized its significance and had with him the many able scientists, including Frisch and Meitner, he had driven out of Germany during the preceding years.

THE START OF NUCLEAR WEAPONS RESEARCH

As it happened, the discovery was published to the world, and almost immediately confirmed by many other groups of scientists. Soon after, its potentialities were foreseen by some leading American and British scientists and, in view of the worsening international situation, they agreed to suspend further publication of their results.

Early British work

In Britain, a Committee was set up under the chairmanship of Professor Sir George Thomson to study the feasibility of developing this discovery into a usable weapon. Some of the critical preliminary experiments were made at Imperial College in London and at Liverpool University, and calculations undertaken, notably by Professor R. E. Peierls, himself a refugee from Germany. Their conclusions were optimistic; they thought a bomb could be made, but realized that it would require immense industrial effort that could not be undertaken in Britain, whose economy was already strained to the limit in those critical years.[1]

The scientists in the United States were kept fully informed of this work. As the war progressed, the main British effort was concentrated on the gaseous diffusion process under the direction of Sir Francis Simon at Oxford. In 1942, it was decided to concentrate the atomic bomb work in the United States, and many of the British scientists joined their American colleagues and worked with them for the duration of the war.

The French contribution

Before France was overrun, important work on the nuclear properties of heavy water was being done by Halban and Kowarski in Paris. They managed to escape to Britain, bringing with them their precious stock of about forty gallons of heavy water. They worked for a time in Cambridge, and then transferred to Canada, where they played an important part in establishing the heavy water reactor at Chalk River.[2]

Work in the United States

In the United States, activity was no less intense. Many of the leading physicists had only recently escaped from Nazi tyranny, and knew that German scientists were already working towards a nuclear bomb. They realized that if they succeeded in putting this weapon into Hitler's hands first, he would be in a position to conquer the world, and would not respect the neutrality of the United States any more than he did that of the countries he had overrun in Europe. Already there was news of intensive work on fission in Berlin, and later this was underlined by the Nazi's interest in the heavy water plant in Norway. Daring Anglo-Norwegian Commando raids were made on this plant, and a ship carrying most of

[1] Sir George Thomson, "Anglo-U.S. Cooperation on Atomic Energy", *ASN*, 2, 345 (1953); R. W. Clark, *The Birth of the Bomb*, Phoenix, London, 1961.

[2] J. Allier, "The First Atomic Piles and the French Effort", *ASN*, 2, 225 (1953).

the stock of heavy water to Germany was sunk. It turned out later that the German efforts to make the atomic bomb were comparatively lethargic and unsuccessful, but to the Allies in the early stages of the war the possibility of the Nazis making the first atomic bomb had to be taken very seriously indeed.[3]

The leading American nuclear physicists agreed to carry on with their researches into fission and to impress on their Government the urgency of the work. In March 1939, Professor G. B. Pegram, supported by Fermi and Szilard, wrote to Admiral S. C. Hooper, director of the technical division of naval operations. His letter noted that uranium might possibly be used as an explosive a million times as powerful as those currently in use. It had little effect, for in those days the Services were not well prepared to appreciate the potentialities of the new scientific developments.[4]

As the studies of fission progressed, the prospects of achieving a chain reaction became more and more promising, and the scientists were increasingly alarmed at the inactivity of the Government. They decided that a direct approach to President Roosevelt would have the best chance of success, and they chose Albert Einstein to make it on their behalf. Szilard and Wigner, two leading physicists, drafted the letter, and it was sent to the President on August 2nd, 1939. As a result of this letter a Committee was appointed to look into the matter. In November, it decided that the researches deserved Government support, and made a grant of $6,000 for the following year. This sum was quite insufficient, but fortunately scientists managed to continue their work with the substantial support of their own universities.

[3] S. A. Goudsmit, "How Germany lost the Race", *BAS*, *1*, 7, 4 (1946); "Heisenberg on the German Uranium Project", *BAS*, *3*, 343 (1947); *ALSOS*, Sigma Books, London; *BAS*, *3*, 354 (1947); M. von Laue, "The Wartime Activities of German Scientists", *BAS*, *4*, 103 (1948); N. Kurti, "The Search for the German Atom Bomb", *ASN*, *1*, 182 (1948).

[4] A. H. Compton, *Atomic Quest*, pp. 25 *et seq*. Many of the details in this chapter are taken from this admirable and absorbing book.

They realized that the Government was quite unprepared to mobilize the forces of science for the coming war. Dr Vannevar Bush, a respected and influential scientist, discussed the matter with Roosevelt, and as a result the National Defense Research Committee was formed to correlate research in fields of military importance, excluding aeronautics. This committee took over responsibility for the fission research, and soon the Government support was being measured in hundreds of thousands of dollars.

There were then three main lines of research that could lead to an atomic bomb. Fermi was working at Columbia to try to achieve a chain reaction in natural uranium. E. O. Lawrence, inventor of the cyclotron, was using his new 5,000-ton model to separate small quantities of the fissile U235 from natural uranium, while Urey was studying separation by the diffusion process. In January 1941, Allison began using the Chicago cyclotron to measure the effects of neutrons on various nuclei, which had to be known for future work, particularly for the choice of the best moderator. In addition, there were some early studies of the possible application of nuclear fission to ship propulsion. It was soon realized that this could not be done quickly enough to affect the course of the war, so the work was suspended for the duration.

Doubts and hesitations

This work was promising, but it was still by no means certain that the energy of uranium could ever be liberated explosively, or that if it could be done a usable weapon would be ready in time to influence the course of the war. It became clear that the work should either be intensified or abandoned for the duration of the war. A committee was set up in April 1941, with Professor A. H. Compton as Chairman, to assess the military value of nuclear energy. It reached the conclusion that research should be intensified to settle the question one way or the other, but that whatever the outcome atomic bombs could not be expected before 1945.

The outlook was not particularly hopeful, and the whole programme came very close to being dropped. Even if Fermi got his chain reaction going, it was not clear how it could be made into a bomb. The amounts of U235 separated by the cyclotron were minute, and the diffusion work was held up by the difficulty of finding a suitable porous barrier. The situation was changed as soon as it was realized that the Fermi pile could be used to make the new fissile element plutonium, which could be extracted chemically. Here at last was a process that could be developed industrially on a large scale with good prospects of success. At this critical moment, Dr M. L. E. Oliphant visited the United States with news of the latest British work which showed that much less U235 would be needed for a chain reaction than had been thought previously. Fermi calculated that about a hundred pounds of fissile material, U235 or plutonium, would be enough for a nuclear explosion.

It was still very difficult to estimate the destructive power of the bomb, how long it would take to make it and at what cost. At a meeting in October 1941, the experts were very reluctant to make any estimates, but the general opinion was that it could be done in three to five years at a cost of some hundreds of millions of dollars; in the event, these estimates turned out to be remarkably accurate. In the same month, Pegram and Urey visited England and were greatly impressed by the work being done, and the favourable views of most leading British physicists. The information they took back with them encouraged the American physicists to continue their work.

By this time, both the American and the British scientists were convinced of the feasibility of the bomb. A full report was transmitted to the President in November 1941, and immediate authorization was given to intensify further studies. If a favourable report could be made within six months a full-scale programme with all the available resources of American industry would follow.

The major effort begins

From then on events moved rapidly. All branches of the research effort were speeded up. The chemistry of plutonium was extensively studied, and preliminary sketches made of the huge plants necessary to produce it in the required quantities. Exceptionally pure materials were made on a large scale for Fermi's pile, and a variety of electronic instruments prepared. The hazards of the high levels of radioactivity were not overlooked and health physicists were appointed and remote handling techniques developed.

The progress made by the different research teams was critically evaluated. Urey's work on the diffusion process was going well, apart from the difficulty of finding a suitable porous barrier, and so was Lawrence's electromagnetic separation. Fermi was steadily continuing his work at Columbia.

The favourable report was made, and preparations for full-scale production began. The problems were formidable, and professional engineers were called in to take over from the research scientists. In June 1942, the U.S. Corps of Engineers was given the ultimate responsibility of producing plutonium and U235.

Fermi's pile

The work on plutonium was moved to Chicago, and extensive metallurgical studies began. Fermi took over a disused squash court and began to build his pile with the increasing quantities of the very pure materials that soon became available. Wigner and Wheeler worked on the design of the production plant. Natural uranium, until then a rare metal produced in small quantities, was needed in ever-growing amounts and chemical plants were set up to produce it. The climax came on December 2nd, 1942, when Fermi's pile "went critical" for the first time, showing the essential practicability of the whole method.[5]

[5] A. H. Compton, "The Birth of Nuclear Power", *BAS*, 9, 10 (1953).

THE PRODUCTION OF BOMBS

Apart from the efforts to produce fissile material, it was also necessary to discover how best to make it into a usable bomb as soon as it became available. Some preliminary studies were made in 1941 and 1942 by Professor G. Breit. It was necessary to attain some understanding of the way the fission process would turn into an explosion. How could the sub-critical mass of fissile material be made critical, and for how long would the chain reaction continue before the uranium was blown to pieces? How much damage would be done by an explosion in which a given number of uranium nuclei underwent fission?

This was a task for the theoretical physicists, and they found in Professor J. Robert Oppenheimer a man well able to lead and coordinate their work. He was not only a physicist of high ability, with a flair for seizing the essentials of a problem, but could inspire the confidence and cooperation of those who came to work with him. Seldom have such a distinguished group of men devoted all their energies to the solution of a single problem. They included Edward Teller whose brilliant ideas came in a continuous stream and Hans Bethe whose encyclopedic knowledge enabled him to select from among them those worthy of practical study. They were joined by Peierls from England and by Fermi from Chicago as soon as his pile experiments were brought to their successful conclusion.

Los Alamos

Oppenheimer selected Los Alamos, on a remote mesa thirty miles from Santa Fé, as the site of his laboratory.[6] They moved into Los Alamos in March 1943 and so rapidly was the work pushed ahead that within four months they had

[6] B. Brode, "Life at Los Alamos, 1943–45", *ASJ*, *3*, 87 (1953); J. R. Oppenheimer, *BAS*, *10*, 181 (1954); N. E. Bradbury, "The Los Alamos Laboratory", *BAS*, *10*, 358 (1954); J. H. Manley, "The Los Alamos Scientific Laboratory", *BAS*, *5*, 101 (1949).

a cyclotron installed and producing on the spot the data needed for their calculations. By the time the fissile material arrived in bulk, Oppenheimer's team knew how to make it into bombs.

Plutonium production

In the autumn of 1942, the Du Pont Company joined the plutonium project with the responsibility of constructing the full-scale production plant. A site was chosen near Hanford on the Columbia River, which provided cooling water for the reactors. A pilot plant was built at Oak Ridge, and studies made of the best way of making the uranium rods and coating them with aluminium so that they would not be corroded by the cooling water. Construction of the Hanford plant began early in 1943. Upwards of fifty thousand workers were employed, and every effort was made to bring it into operation as soon as possible.

A group of chemists under G. Seaborg studied the chemistry of plutonium, working with the microscopic amounts produced by the pilot plant. As soon as the reactors at Hanford began to operate, the extraction of plutonium from the uranium rods began. Sufficient was obtained by 1945 for use in the bomb on Nagasaki.

In peacetime only one of the many processes for producing fissile material would have been selected for industrial development. But with the urgency of war economic considerations had to take second place and all the feasible methods were developed to the full, just in case unforeseen difficulties prevented the completion of one or other of them.

A giant magnet was built at Oak Ridge, Tennessee, to separate U235 from natural uranium by the electromagnetic process. It needed large quantities of copper for its windings, but copper was in short supply due to the demands of the war effort. So silver from the U.S. Treasury was used instead, fifteen thousand tons of it.

A full-scale plant was also built at Oak Ridge for U235

separation by the gaseous diffusion process. By the time it was finished it was the largest continuous process plant in the world, cost several hundred million dollars, covered an area half a mile long and a quarter of a mile wide, and required as much power to run as New York. It was filled with intricate systems of pipes and pumps to push the gaseous uranium hexafluoride again and again through porous barriers, each time effecting a minute degree of separation. Experience showed this to be the most efficient way of separating U235, so the electromagnetic separation plant was finally closed down. Further gaseous diffusion plants have since been built at Portsmouth and Paducah in the United States, and at Capenhurst in Great Britain. The Hiroshima bomb was made from U235 separated in this way.

The Alamogordo test

In the spring of 1945, U235 from Oak Ridge and plutonium from Hanford began to arrive at Los Alamos in substantial amounts. The procedure for making the fissile material into a bomb had been worked out by Oppenheimer's teams. On July 16th, the first test was made near Alamogordo in New Mexico. It was a complete success. The theoretical predictions were verified, and the long labours of thousands of scientists and engineers were at last rewarded. Within a month the second and third bombs were dispatched to the Pacific where, at Hiroshima and Nagasaki, they reduced thriving cities to desolate wastes, killed or maimed over a hundred thousand Japanese, and brought the war with Japan to an abrupt end.

In the following years many more test explosions were made, starting with those at Bikini Atoll,[7] and continuing

---

[7] *BAS*, *1*, 11, 7 (1946); *BAS*, *2*, 3–4, 26 (1946); "Atomic Tests" *BAS*, *9*, 85 (1953). There was some public concern in connection with the early tests about the possibility of initiating a chain reaction in the air or the sea. This fear can be shown to be groundless. See H. A. Bethe, "Can Air or Water be Exploded?", *BAS*, *1*, 7, 2 (1946).

there and in the Nevada desert, in order to produce more efficient and powerful bombs.

THERMONUCLEAR WEAPONS

During the time the fission bombs were being developed, very little attention was paid to the other theoretically feasible method of releasing nuclear energy, that by the fusion of light nuclei. But a few men, notably Professor E. Teller, kept thinking about the possibility of making a fusion bomb, vastly more powerful than the fission bomb.[8]

The principles of fusion had been understood for a long time. If hydrogen isotopes, like deuterium and tritium, collide violently, they are likely to fuse together, with enormous energy release. This fusion can only be brought about on a large scale if the whole mass of hydrogen is heated so that energetic collisions are continually taking place between the particles comprising it.[9] Unfortunately, the temperature required before the fusion reaction starts is 300 million degrees for deuterium alone, and 50 million degrees for a mixture of deuterium and tritium, far beyond any attainable by man at that time. Such temperatures only exist inside stars, where thermonuclear reactions continually take place and provide most of their energy.

The situation was changed by the fission bomb, which provided a means of attaining the high temperatures required. The fission bomb could thus be used as a detonator, raising the mixture of hydrogen isotopes to the temperature at which the fusion reaction can begin. However, it was not certain that the temperature would be high enough for the fusion reaction, unless a considerable proportion of the very expensive[10] tritium was used. In 1945 the whole project was doubtful, and work on it came practically to an end with the

[8] *BAS, 10*, 287 (1954).
[9] H. A. Bethe, "The Hydrogen Bomb", *BAS, 6*, 99 (1950); L. Ridenour, "The Physics of the H-Bomb", *BAS, 6*, 105 (1950).
[10] About a million dollars per pound.

reduction of activity at Los Alamos following the end of the war.

The project was thoroughly studied in 1949 at a meeting of the General Advisory Committee of the U.S. Atomic Energy Commission, composed of leading nuclear physicists. The outlook was uncertain, but the Committee expressed the view that "an imaginative and concerted attack on the problem has a better than even chance of producing the weapon within five years".[11] Soon after, on January 31st, 1950, President Truman directed the A.E.C. to continue its weapons research including that on the hydrogen bomb.[12]

Teller's breakthrough

By the middle of 1950 the research seemed to have reached a deadlock. The prospects seemed less and less promising,[13] and it looked as if there was a long hard row ahead.[14] Then, in the spring of 1951, Teller made a brilliant discovery which changed the whole picture. Until then it had been mostly speculation and groping in the dark; afterwards, the way ahead was clear, and the work could be pushed ahead with a definite technical programme that seemed bound to succeed. Progress was rapid, and by May 25th, 1951, the A.E.C. was able to announce that a series of weapons tests had been made at Eniwetok Atoll including "experiments contributing to thermonuclear weapons research".[15]

The Eniwetok test

In June 1951, the leading scientists, including Oppenheimer, Bethe, Teller, Fermi, Wheeler, Bacher, Bradbury

[11] *In the Matter of J. Robert Oppenheimer: I. Transcript of Hearing before Personnel Security Board*, U.S.A.E.C., 1954, p. 228. H. A. Bethe, *op. cit.*, p. 330; M. A. Kelly, *op. cit.*, p. 64; *BAS, 10*, 289 (1954).

[12] *BAS, 6*, 66 (1950). For ensuing discussion in Britain and the U.S., see *ASN, 3*, 76 and 110 (1950). See also R. F. Bacher, "The Hydrogen Bomb", *ASN, 3*, 134 (1950); H. Thirring, "The Super Bomb", *BAS, 6*, 69 (1950); R. Sawyer, "The H-bomb Chronology", *BAS, 10*, 287 (1954).

[13] H. A. Bethe, *op. cit.*, p. 330.

[14] J. R. Oppenheimer, *op. cit.*, pp. 83 *et seq.*

[15] "The Eniwetok Tests", *BAS, 7*, 239 (1951).

and von Neumann met at Princeton to review the progress that had been made. The weapon now seemed quite feasible, and steps were taken to prepare for a full-scale test.[16] The whole complex process of designing a workable bomb from the basic ideas to the actual thing was carried out with remarkable speed, and the first H-bomb was exploded at Eniwetok in November 1952.[17] A still more powerful type was exploded at Bikini Atoll in March 1954.

The early version of the H-bomb used deuterium and tritium in their liquid form. As they are gases at normal temperatures they have to be cooled greatly and compressed before they liquefy. The bomb thus needed a considerable amount of liquefying apparatus. The first thermonuclear device probably weighed some tens of tons, and could hardly be considered a practicable weapon.

Later, lithium 6 deuteride was used as the main constituent. Lithium is the third lightest type of nucleus and can react with neutrons to give tritium. The tritium is thus made continuously on the spot, which is much more convenient, and also lithium deuteride is a solid so that the liquefying apparatus is no longer needed. This forms the basis of a compact weapon that can be delivered by air.

The Bikini test and the Lucky Dragon

The test explosion at Bikini on March 1st, 1954, was the most powerful man-made explosion up to that time, being equivalent to about fifteen million tons, or megatons, of T.N.T. Even though fifty thousand square miles of the Pacific Ocean had been declared a test area and prohibited to shipping, its effects were widely experienced elsewhere. Due to a sudden change in wind, radioactive dust was showered on the islands of Rongelap, Rongerik and Uterik

[16] "The Hidden Struggle for the H-bomb", *ASJ*, *3*, 142 (1954).
[17] A. G. W. Cameron, "Multiple Neutron Capture in the 'Mike' Fusion Explosion", *Canadian Journal of Physics*, *37*, 322 (1959); *ASN*, *2*, 212 (1953); "The 'Hydrogen Bomb' Story", *BAS*, *8*, 297 (1952).

and the inhabitants had to be hurriedly evacuated.[18] A Japanese fishing boat, about eighty to a hundred miles from the explosion, was showered with radioactive dust.[19] The crew soon felt unwell and they decided to return to Japan. Several of them became seriously ill and one of them subsequently died.[20] Thousands of tons of tuna fish landed in Japan were found to be radioactive and had to be destroyed.

These and other unfortunate events enabled independent scientists to make a study of the explosion products. Several Japanese, in particular, were able to collect radioactive dust from the exposed fishing boats, and some of them detected its presence in rain for weeks after the explosion.[21] The dust was analysed and found to contain the usual range of fission products. This was to be expected from a hydrogen bomb since a fission bomb is used to start the fusion reaction. But when the quantity of fission products was estimated, it turned out to be far too high. The calculations were inevitably rough, but they indicated that the major part of the energy of the supposed thermonuclear explosion in fact came from fission. There was much more of the fission products than could be accounted for by the detonation alone.

The fission-fusion-fission bomb

Professor Rotblat, to whom Professor Nishiwaki had shown his results, realized the explanation.[22] The power of the hydrogen bomb had been boosted by surrounding the thermonuclear core with a shell of U238, which undergoes fission

[18] "The H-Bomb and World Opinion", *BAS*, *10*, 163 (1954); "A Navy Medical Team Studies Fall-out Effects", *BAS*, *12*, 58 (1956).

[19] R. A. Lapp, *The Voyage of the Lucky Dragon*, Penguin Books, No. 195, 1957.

[20] J. R. Arnold, "Effects of the Recent Bomb Tests on Human Beings", *BAS*, *10*, 347 (1954); "Radiation Exposures in Recent Weapons Tests", *BAS*, *10*, 352 (1954).

[21] Y. Nishiwaki, "Bikini Ash", *ASJ*, *4*, 97 (1954). "The Bikini Hydrogen Bomb Tests", *ASJ*, *4*, 50 (1954); *3*, 292 (1954); *BAS*, *10*, 234 (1954).

[22] J. Rotblat, "The Hydrogen-Uranium Bomb", *ASJ*, *4*, 224 (1955); J. M. Fowler, *Fall-Out*, Basic Books, New York, 1960, p. 17.

like U235 when hit by the *fast* neutrons produced in enormous
numbers by the thermonuclear reaction. It is thus a three-
stage reaction: the U235 or plutonium fission reaction starts
with slow neutrons, and the intense heat ignites the thermonuclear reaction. This produces fast neutrons that cause yet
more fissions in the surrounding U238. Since the U238 is an
unused by-product of the process separating the fissile U235,
the extra power of the "three-decker" fission-fusion-fission
bomb is obtained at hardly any extra cost. A secondary effect
of the U238 is that it acts as a tamper in keeping the reacting
mass together for a little longer, thus increasing the power
again.

The cobalt bomb

Previously, there had been some discussion of the possibility of rigging an ordinary H-bomb with some material, like
cobalt, which is made intensely radioactive by the explosion.[23]
This radioactive material, spread over a wide area, would
greatly add to the destructiveness of the bomb. The development of the "three-decker" bomb renders this obsolete, because it gives not only the extra radioactivity, but also vastly
greater destructive power.

THE NUCLEAR ARMS RACE

In the following years, intensive work on the bombs continued in order to make them more compact and efficient.
Atomic bombs were so reduced in size that they can now be
fired from a gun or carried by a small rocket, and so tactical
atomic weapons have augmented the firepower of modern
armies.[24] Work on the hydrogen bomb has been mainly
directed to making them "clean", that is, to reduce the pro-

[23] *ASJ*, *5*, 267 (1956); J. R. Arnold, "The Hydrogen-Cobalt Bomb",
BAS, *6*, 290 (1950).
[24] T. R. Phillips, "The Atomic Revolution in Warfare", *BAS*, *10*,
315 (1954); G. C. Reinhardt and W. R. Kintner, "The Tactical Side
of Atomic Warfare", *BAS*, *11*, 53 (1955).

portion of their explosive power derived from the fission detonator, that gives unwanted radioactive fall-out. Hydrogen bombs that are 90 per cent clean have now been produced.[25]

Many other countries have entered the nuclear arms race. Russia exploded its first atomic bomb in September 1949[26] and its first hydrogen bomb on August 12th, 1953.[27] Great Britain followed with an atomic bomb on October 3rd, 1952,[28] and a hydrogen bomb on May 15th, 1957, and France exploded an atomic bomb on February 14th, 1960. These initial explosions have been followed by a long series of tests to aid the development of improved types of bombs.

THE OPPENHEIMER CASE

The intensified decade of research that culminated in the explosion of the first hydrogen bomb had to be carried out in the strictest secrecy. During the war years it was imperative to conceal the new developments from the Nazis, and unfortunately it did not prove possible to relax this secrecy in the post-war years. Scientists, who are used to full and free publication and discussion of their work, do not take easily to secrecy, but they were willing to observe it in the interests of national security. It was, however, inevitable that a tension should arise between the military authorities who tended to think that everything should be kept rigidly secret, even at the expense of considerable internal inefficiency, and the scientists who knew that secrecy can do no more than retard developments as it is only a matter of time before other countries discover them for themselves.

This tension came to a head when, towards the end of 1953, Dr J. R. Oppenheimer was informed by Major-General K. D.

[25] J. Maddox, "The 'Clean' Hydrogen Bomb", *NS*, 2, No. 29. 27 (1957); R. E. Lapp, "The 'Humanitarian' H-Bomb", *BAS*, *12*, 261 (1956).

[26] "The Russian Explosion", *BAS*, *5*, 261 (1949).

[27] *BAS*, *9*, 236 (1953).

[28] Sir William Penney, "The Montebello Explosion", *BAS*, *8*, 295 (1952); *ASN*, 2, 151, 200 (1953).

Nichols, general manager of the Atomic Energy Commission, that in view of certain Communist associations, mostly previous to his work on the atomic bomb, and of his alleged opposition to the H-bomb programme, his employment on A.E.C. work and access to restricted data were suspended. His case was fully investigated by the Gray Board between April 12th and May 6th, 1954, and numerous scientists of high distinction testified on his behalf. The Board concluded that Dr Oppenheimer was a loyal citizen, but in view of his associations and conduct on a number of occasions recommended that his clearance be not reinstated. One of the three members of the Board, Dr W. Evans, dissented from the verdict. The case was reconsidered by the five A.E.C. Commissioners, who upheld the verdict, with Dr H. D. Smyth dissenting.

The whole affair shocked many scientists, and most of them considered that Dr Oppenheimer had been unjustly subjected to a cruel ordeal, and unwisely prevented from continuing his invaluable services to the A.E.C. Others, notably Teller, considered that the thermonuclear bomb programme had not been pushed forward as rapidly as it might have been, and that the suspension of Oppenheimer's security clearance was justified. The Oppenheimer case brought home to scientists the hazards of giving advice even on purely scientific matters, and the widely varying concepts of security against which their actions would be judged.[29]

[29] For detailed accounts of the Oppenheimer Case, and comments upon it, see:

In the Matter of J. Robert Oppenheimer: I. Transcript of Hearing before Personnel Security Board; II. Texts of Principal Documents and Letters of Personnel Security Board, General Manager, Commissioners, U.S. Government Printing Office, Washington, D.C., 1954; "Nichols presents Charges", BAS, 10, 174 (1954); "Oppenheimer Replies", BAS, 10, 177 (1954); "Scientists Affirm Faith in Oppenheimer", BAS, 10, 188 (1954); R. E. Peierls, ASJ, 4, 145 (1955); H. Kalven, BAS, 10, 259 (1954); "A.E.C. Majority Decision", BAS, 10, 275 (1954); R. Sawyer, "More than Security", BAS, 10, 284 (1954); N. S. Finney, "The Threat to Atomic Science", BAS, 10, 285 (1954);

BAS, 10, 234 (1954); *BAS, 10,* 387 (1954); C. P. Curtis, *The Oppenheimer Case: The Trial of a Security System,* New York, Simon and Schuster, 1955; A. M. Schlesinger, *Harper's Monthly,* October 1954; editorials in *Discovery* (November 1954) and *Nature* (September 25th, 1954), J. Rotblat, *ASJ, 5,* 196 (1956).

Many other scientists in the United States were affected by similar charges: B. S. Miller and H. S. Brown, "Loyalty Procedures of the A.E.C.—A Report and Recommendation", *BAS, 4,* 45 (1948). "Loyalty Clearance Procedures in Research Laboratories", *BAS, 4,* 111 (1948); J. L. O'Brian, "Loyalty Tests and Guilt by Association", *BAS, 4,* 166 (1948). See also *BAS, 4,* 173, 193, 226, 281, 290, 342, 373 (1948); *5,* 162, 298, 337 (1949); *6,* 32, 34, 333 (1950); *7,* 323, 346, 355 (1951); *9,* 3, 211, 229 (1953); *11,* 65 (1955); M. Marder, *The Fort Monmouth Story, 10,* 21 (1954); E. Shils, *BAS, 11,* 106, 196, 247 (1955); *12,* 227 (1956); *14,* 80 (1958); R. S. Brown, *Loyalty and Security Employment Tests in the U.S.,* Yale U.P., 1958, *BAS, 14,* 276 (1958); L. N. Ridenour, *BAS, 1,* No. 6, 3 (1946); B. J. Bok, F. Friedman and V. F. Weisskopf, "Security Regulations in the Field of Nuclear Research", *BAS, 3,* 321 (1947). "How Far Should Military Censorship Extend?", *BAS, 4,* 163 (1948).

The Oppenheimer case must be considered in the context of the widespread spying undertaken by agents of the Soviet Union. See "Soviet Atomic Espionage", *ASN, 1,* 111 (1952). *BAS, 7,* 143 (1951); "The Fuchs Case", *BAS, 6,* 68 (1950); E. Rabinowitch, "Atomic Spy Trials", *BAS, 7,* 139 (1951); H. De Wolf Smyth, "Science and Secrecy", *ASJ, 3,* 67 (1953).

CHAPTER III

BIOLOGICAL EFFECTS OF NUCLEAR RADIATIONS

Radioactivity was discovered by Becquerel in 1896, when he found that a photographic plate was fogged by rays from a uranium salt even when it was wrapped in black paper. Pierre and Marie Curie tried to isolate the substances that emitted this type of radiation and eventually discovered radium. Becquerel carried some radium in a glass tube in his waistcoat pocket for several days, and noticed that it caused a small burn on his skin. This is the first recorded instance of biological damage due to nuclear radiation. Pierre Curie made a systematic study of the effect of the rays from radium on the skin of his own arm, and found that they were able to produce quite severe burns.

X-rays, discovered by Roentgen in 1895, had already been found to have similar effects.[1] Many of the early users of X-ray tubes for medical diagnosis suffered from burns on their hands and arms, and frequently lost their fingers and died prematurely. A study of over 82,000 American medical men who died between 1930 and 1954 showed that, on the

---

[1] Strictly speaking, X-rays are not nuclear radiations since they arise from transitions between low-lying electronic energy levels outside the nucleus. However, since they have the same nature as the nuclear gamma rays, both being electromagnetic radiations, it is convenient to consider them together for the present purpose.

average, radiologists had their lives shortened by over five years compared with the rest of the profession.[2]

RADIATION HAZARDS

None of these radiations can be detected by our senses, so we are not alerted to the danger as we are, for example, when we touch a hot object. We could receive a fatal dose of radiation without being aware of anything unusual. The effects appear sooner or later, depending on the intensity of the exposure. A severe irradiation will rapidly cause irritation and smarting of the skin, while very small exposures may not cause visible effects for years or even decades.

These two characteristics of nuclear radiations, their not being recorded by the senses and their delayed action effects, undoubtedly hindered recognition of the harm they can do. Nevertheless, some at least of the harmful effects were soon recognized, and as early as 1896 Elihu Thomson drew up an effective set of rules for preventing injury by radiation.

X-rays

In spite of this, very many early X-ray sets were quite inadequately shielded, and the dangerous nature of the radiation was not understood by the operators. An ordinary routine X-ray examination of the chest, for example, does not need a high intensity, and the damage can be reduced to negligible proportions. It is important to ensure that no other parts of the body are unnecessarily exposed, and that the operators are well shielded. They are continually present during many exposures and could, over a period of time, accumulate a dangerous dose even if the exposure during each individual X-ray was quite small. Neglect of these precautions has frequently led to severe injuries. Nowadays the

[2] J. Schubert and R. E. Lapp, *Radiation: What it is and how it affects you*, London, Heinemann, and New York, Viking Press, 1957, p. 90. Many of the facts quoted in this chapter were obtained from this informative book.

most careful precautions are taken to eliminate unnecessary irradiation, but injuries still occur, and it may be questioned whether more could not still be done to minimize exposure to X-rays.

Radioactive materials

A similar story could be told for the effects of radioactive substances. These emit three types of rays, called alpha, beta and gamma. The alpha rays are nuclei of helium and, since they are doubly charged, ionize heavily and are soon brought to rest. Most of them are stopped by the dead outer layers of the skin and so do not constitute a serious hazard so long as the radioactive material is outside the body. The beta rays consist of fast electrons which can penetrate a little way into the body, where they cause slight ionization. The gamma rays are more penetrating and can cause damage through the ionization they produce inside the body.

Radium

On the whole, radioactive materials, unless specially concentrated, are unlikely to cause much harm as long as they remain outside the body. If, however, they are inhaled as dust particles or ingested in food, the heavily ionizing alpha particles can cause serious damage. Since radium is chemically similar to calcium, one of the main constituents of bones, it is sent by the body to the bone matrix. Here it can bombard the tissues that make the white blood cells, our chief safeguards against bacterial infection. As the half-life of radium is extremely long, 1,600 years, it does not appreciably diminish in intensity with time. Plutonium, with a half-life of 24,000 years, is equally dangerous. These substances are far more toxic than the most deadly chemical poison; the fatal dose of plutonium, for example, is a few thousandths of a gram, a speck of dust too small to be seen. Weight for weight, radium is 25,000 times more deadly than arsenic.

Early radiation injuries

This type of radiation injury usually takes years to develop, and so in many tragic cases the damage was irreparably done long before any symptoms became apparent. A notorious case is that of the girls who, during and after the First World War, painted the dials of luminous clocks with paint containing radium. To get a sharp point on them, they frequently licked their brushes, and so absorbed minute amounts of radium. Years later these girls, many of them married with families, experienced pains in the jaw, followed gradually and inexorably by the progressive deterioration of the body characteristic of radium poisoning. One of them died of cancer of the bone in 1944, twenty-six years after she stopped dial painting. Another died a lingering death, "a helpless, blind invalid, racked with pain, unable even to mumble a few words to her husband". This was caused by a few millionths of a gram of radium.[3]

Far from being shunned as a deadly poison, radium was hailed by many medical men as the cure for numerous ills. Thousands of people rich enough to afford the "cure" drank solutions containing radium salts. In 1916 it was stated in the journal *Radium* that "radium has absolutely no toxic effects, it being accepted as harmoniously by the human system as is sunlight by the plant". The experiences of the dial painters altered this view, and now one rarely hears of the life-giving properties of radium solutions. In atomic energy plants, where large quantities of plutonium are continually handled, the most careful safety procedures are enforced to prevent injuries.[4]

THE MECHANISM OF RADIATION DAMAGE

These damaging effects of nuclear radiations may be understood if their action on living tissue is examined in more

[3] J. Schubert and R. E. Lapp, *op. cit.*, p. 109.

[4] W. G. Marley and J. E. Johnston, "Health Physics Aspects of the Atomic Energy Programme", *NS*, 5, 1137 (1959); "Atomic Review: The safest industry", *Engineering*, *189*, 691 (1960).

detail. The unit of living tissue is the cell, a complex, self-reproducing system composed of many millions of extremely large and complex molecules. Each part of the cell is delicately adjusted to play its part in the life of the whole. In a similar way groups of cells form a tissue, the tissues organs, and the organs in turn subserve the whole body.

When nuclear radiation, for example an alpha particle, tears through this hierarchy of biological systems, a number of disruptive effects are set in motion. Individual atoms may be knocked out of molecules, thus changing their behaviour or even breaking them up. The electric field of the alpha particle can eject electrons from molecules, forming highly reactive ions and free radicals. These can travel through the cell and react with more molecules, breaking them up in turn. The passage of a single alpha particle can thus affect hundreds of thousands of molecules.

The number of molecules in a cell, however, is so large that unless a vital part is hit the normal repair mechanism of the cell is apparently able to make good the damage. But if a tissue is exposed to a continuous bombardment for many years, as can happen if radioactive material is lodged in a nearby bone, the resistance of the cells is gradually worn down and permanent damage can occur. The same happens if a tissue is exposed to a massive dose in a very short time. The damage caused by a definite amount of radiation depends on the period over which it is delivered, due to the repair processes that operate in the cells. Thus a single large dose could cause detectable damage, while the same dose spread over a number of years would not be noticeable.

Dosage measurement

In order to make possible a quantitative study of the effects of different doses and types of radiation, a unit of dosage, called the roentgen, has been defined. It is a measure of the amount of ionization produced in the tissue, and is such that one roentgen, delivered to a cubic centimetre of standard air, produces two billion ion pairs. The energy delivered is sufficient to separate this number of electrons from their parent atoms. To put the number in perspective, this may be compared with the total number of atoms in a cubic centimetre of air, which is so large that one roentgen unit only ionizes one atom in ten billion. This unit was originally defined for X-rays and gamma rays only. A similar unit, the rad, has been defined for alpha and beta particles; it corresponds to the absorption of a hundred ergs of energy per gram of air. Since a roentgen delivers about eighty-four ergs per gram, the two units are very roughly the same.

Another important unit is the curie, defined as the radioactivity of one gram (one-twenty-eighth of an ounce) of radium. This unit of radioactivity may be extended to other radioactive substances by defining a curie as the amount of that substance that has the same number of disintegrations per second, about thirty-seven billion, as a gram of radium. For most purposes, the curie is an inconveniently large unit, so the millicurie and the microcurie, one-thousandth and one-millionth of a curie respectively, are often used instead. Similar subdivisions are made of the roentgen and the rad.

Types of radiation damage

The damage done by a given dose depends on the type of radiation causing the ionization.[5] Thus beta and gamma rays spread their ionization over a large volume, so that the amount in any particular region may be small enough to be counteracted by the normal repair processes. Alpha particles, on the other hand, deliver their radiation in such concentrated amounts in small regions that the repair processes are frequently unable to cope with the disruptive effects and the cell dies. This difference between the effects of the same dose of radiation delivered by different types of radiations is described by the relative biological effectiveness (RBE) of the radiations.

[5] R. C. Hoyt, "What is Radiation?" *BAS, 14*, 9 (1958).

The RBE of alpha particles is about twenty times that of X-rays and gamma rays.

The effect of a given dose also depends on the tissue irradiated; some are more sensitive than others. A dose of several hundred roentgens on the arm would cause much less damage than the same dose on the body. In general, growing tissues containing many reproducing cells are particularly sensitive, while those whose growth is complete are not nearly so sensitive. Thus the bone marrow, ceaselessly producing new white blood corpuscles to fight infection, is much more sensitive than muscle and skin, and children are more sensitive than adults.

Natural radiation exposure

The human body is continually exposed to small amounts of radiation from exterior and interior sources.[6] The main interior sources are radioactive potassium, carbon and radium. There are about five ounces of potassium in the average adult body, and about one ten-thousandth of this is the radioactive K^{40}. The radioactivity of this is about a tenth of a microcurie, which delivers an internal dose of about 20 millirads per year. Another radioactive element present in the body is carbon 14, the isotope that is extensively used for dating archaeological specimens.[7] The dose due to this element is about 2 millirads per year.

The amounts of these two radioelements in the body can be quite accurately estimated because they both occur as small but definite proportions of elements that are always present in the body in quite substantial amounts. It is otherwise with radium, which occurs in minute and very variable quantities in a wide range of materials, depending on the radium, uranium and thorium content of the soil and rocks.

---

[6] The annual background dose is about 0·134 rem (roentgen equivalent man). This is made up of 0·030 rem from cosmic rays, 0·060 from the earth's surface and 0·044 from internal emitters.

[7] W. F. Libby, "The Radio-Carbon Story", *BAS*, **4**, 263 (1948).

These radioactive elements can find their way into our food, and so enter our bodies. Most of this radioactive material is eliminated fairly soon, but some may become permanently lodged in the body, thus adding to the internal radiation. The external natural radiation is due to the radioactive material present in some rocks, and to the cosmic radiation.

The radiation intensity varies with altitude, dropping quite rapidly for the first few hundred feet above the ground as we get farther away from the radioactivity in the soil, and then gradually increasing again due to the cosmic radiation, whose intensity increases with altitude until far into the stratosphere. At sea level the dose due to the cosmic radiation is about 35 milliroentgens per year, and this dose is roughly doubled for every mile above the earth's surface. The dose due to radioactivity in the rocks varies widely from place to place, and typical values are in the range of 100 to 500 milliroentgens per year. Most of the natural radiation therefore comes from this source.

Additional exposures

Over the last few years, the development of the atomic energy industry and the increasing use of X-rays and radio-isotopes has significantly increased the radiation dose received by the average person. Diagnostic radiology accounts for most of this increase, and so it varies greatly from one person to another. Estimates of the average dose over the whole population vary; for Britain the Medical Research Council[8] has estimated that it amounts to about twenty-two per cent of the natural dose. They found the contributions from other sources to be very much smaller: occupational exposures in radiology and industry about two per cent, luminous clocks

[8] *The Hazards to Man of Nuclear and Allied Radiations*, H.M.S.O. Cmd. 9780. 1956; J. S. Laughlin and R. S. Sherman, "Radiation Exposure Incidental to Medical Practice", *BAS*, *14*, 41 (1958); "Oxford Conference on the Biological Hazards of Atomic Energy", *ASN*, *4*, 56 (1951); J. F. Loutit, "Radiation Hazards of Atomic Energy", *ASJ*, *3*, 321 (1954).

and watches one per cent, shoe-fitting one-tenth of one per cent, television sets much less than one per cent, the Atomic Energy Authority one-tenth of one per cent.[9]

These additional sources of exposure increase the dose we already receive from the natural radiation by a small amount. It is not certain what harm the natural radiation does to us, though it is probably the cause of many cancers. There is evidence that some irreparable injury is caused by any irradiation, however small, and this has the effect of reducing the life span.

The only likely sources of somatic damage, apart from the accidents mentioned above, are occupational exposures and those due to nuclear explosions. The former include those suffered by workers in uranium mines, radiologists and scientists working with isotopes, nuclear reactors and machines producing powerful beams of nuclear particles. With sufficient care, using appropriate masks, shielding and remote handling techniques, these dangers can be virtually eliminated. The safety record of the Atomic Energy Authority is a particularly good one, and so far there have been very few accidents, and none of these proved fatal. The corresponding record of the United States Atomic Energy Commission has been good also, although a few fatal accidents have occurred.[10]

Radiation sickness

When an accident does occur and someone is exposed to a massive dose of radiation severe sickness results, sometimes leading to death. The victim is usually not aware of the exposure when it is actually happening, but some hours or days later, depending on the intensity of the exposure, he will

[9] The UNO Report estimates the dose due to test explosions to be 0·12 rad per generation, compared with 2·5 rads from natural sources and 1–3 rads from X-rays. *Effect of Radiation on Human Heredity*, W.H.O., Geneva, 1957.

[10] L. B. Slotin, *BAS*, *1*, No. 12, 16 (1946); D. Masters, *The Accident*, New York, A. A. Knopf, 1955; G. A. Andrews, "Radiation Accidents", Ch. 7 of *Fall-Out* (Ed. J. M. Fowler), Basic Books, 1960.

experience reddening and irritation of the skin and a general feeling of nausea and malaise. As the radiation sickness develops the resistance of the body to infection decreases because the white blood corpuscles are no longer replenished. Small sores refuse to heal, internal haemorrhages become frequent, and the hair falls out. Fever develops, accompanied by diarrhoea and vomiting. The victim becomes weak and emaciated and gradually falls into a coma and dies. For a severe exposure the whole course of the radiation sickness may take a few weeks. A fatal dose for the average person is in the region of 400 to 600 roentgens. Naturally, a person in excellent health has more chance of survival than one in poor health.[11]

If the dose is less than fatal, or if active measures are taken to combat infection by massive doses of penicillin and by repeated blood transfusions, the initial progress of the sickness follows its usual course, but gradually the fever will be held in check and the blood count restored. Over a period of months the victim's condition will steadily improve and he may be restored to health. It is likely, however, that even if the recovery seems complete there will be some increased susceptibility to leukemia and other forms of cancer, especially in the part of the body where the accidental exposure took place.[12]

In peacetime, such cases of massive radiation exposure are extremely rare, but they would of course be very widespread during a nuclear war. A considerable amount of research has been done on the problem of treating radiation sickness and, if possible, forestalling at least some of its effects. So far, little can be done after the exposure beyond the usual medical treatment, although recently successful results have been obtained by bone transplantation. Some increased resistance to radiation damage has been found if certain substances are

[11] A. M. Brues, "Somatic Effects of Radiation", *BAS*, *14*, 12 (1958).
[12] J. G. Allen, P. V. Moulder and D. M. Enerson, "The Treatment of Irradiation Sickness", *BAS*, *6*, 263 (1950).

taken before the exposure.[13] The aim is to find some chemical that can counteract the devastating effects of the free radicals on the delicate mechanism of the cell. Such a medicine, if it could be perfected, could do no more than reduce the dangers of radiation sickness; it could not eliminate them entirely. It would be useless to guard against accidents, but could be valuable in certain circumstances when the possibility of a massive exposure could be foreseen.

GENETIC EFFECTS OF RADIATION

The genetic effects of nuclear radiations are still far from being fully understood, but much intensive work over the last few decades has established the main facts. The long reproductive period of man and the impracticability of planned experiments make it particularly difficult to gather sufficient data. However, much can be done by observation alone, coupled with a knowledge of family trees that may extend back for several generations. The laws of inheritance first established by experiments on plants, insects and small mammals can then be shown to be consistent with what little we know of man. In this way a sound general picture of the workings of heredity in man has been established, though much still remains to be done.[14]

The laws of heredity: genes

Each human being is formed initially by the union of two cells, the ovum from the mother and the sperm from the father. Each of these cells carries a set of twenty-three

[13] A. Hollaender, "Modification of Radiation Response", *BAS*, *12*, 76 (1956); J. Schubert, "Protection and Treatment", Chs. 5 and 8 in *Fall-Out* (Ed. J. M. Fowler), Basic Books, New York, 1960.
[14] H. Kalmus, *Genetics*, Pelican Books No. A179; E. B. Ford, *Mendelism and Evolution*, and *The Study of Heredity*; H. J. Muller, "Changing Genes: Their Effects on Evolution", *BAS*, *3*, 267 (1947); C. Auerbach, *Genetics in the Atomic Age*, New York: Essential Books Inc., 1956; G. W. Beadle, "Molecules, Viruses and Heredity", *BAS*, *15*, 354 (1959); B. Wallace and Th. Dobzhansky, *Radiation, Genes and Man*, Holt, New York, 1959.

chromosomes which link up with their opposite members from the other cell, producing a fertilized cell with twenty-three pairs of chromosomes. The chromosomes are thread-like structures containing the genes, and the interaction of these genes determines the hereditary constitution of the child. Several pairs of genes may together be responsible for a particular physical characteristic, but it is simpler to think in terms of a one-to-one correspondence between genes and characters.

Thus, for example, there is a well-known gene that determines the eye colour of the child. For the sake of simplicity again, assume that there are only two possible eye colours, brown and blue. There are thus two possible types of eye-colour genes, and a child will receive one from each parent. There are three possible combinations: both blue, both brown and one brown and one blue. If they are both the same colour, this will be the colour of the child's eyes. The interesting case is when the child receives one of each colour. This does not produce a mixture of brown and blue, as might have been expected, but pure brown eyes. This is because the "brown" gene always determines the eye colour, irrespective of the presence of a "blue" gene; we say that the "brown" gene is dominant and the "blue" gene is recessive. Thus a blue-eyed person must have both genes blue, but a brown-eyed person can have either two brown genes or one brown and one blue.

In the next generation, the possessors of similar pairs of genes can only give that gene to their children, but the possessors of one brown and one blue gene can give either a blue gene or a brown gene to their children. Thus blue-eyed parents can only have blue-eyed children, while brown-eyed parents can have children of either eye colour if both parents have one brown and one blue gene. In this case one-quarter of the children, on the average, will have blue eyes. But if either or both parents have two brown genes, all the children will have brown eyes.

It should be pointed out that this is a highly simplified discussion, as there are in fact very many possible eye colours with complex inheritance patterns. This can produce apparent exceptions to the above generalizations. This simple case does, however, bring out some important principles of genetics, particularly the concept of the carrier of a recessive gene. The blue gene is recessive, and it may therefore be inherited and passed on by a brown-eyed person. We only know that he carried the blue gene by its appearance in his children or grandchildren.

The gene is normally a very stable structure, and can survive unchanged from generation to generation for many thousands of years. If it is dominant, it will produce its corresponding physical characteristic or group of characteristics in every person carrying it. If it is recessive, it will only produce its character if the carrier derived the same recessive gene from both its parents.

Mutations

Sometimes a gene is changed or mutated. This can come about for a variety of causes including the action of abnormal temperatures and certain chemical agents. Very often the mutant gene is so radically changed that the cell carrying it will be unable to reproduce itself and dies. If the change is less extensive, the mutant gene may be reproduced just like a normal gene and be handed on to the children. If the new gene is dominant and corresponds to a particular physical characteristic, this will appear in the family for the first time. Much more frequently the mutant gene is recessive, and so may not make its presence apparent for many generations.

In 1927 H. J. Muller, an American geneticist, discovered that X-rays could cause these mutations. He irradiated a large number of fruit flies, *Drosophila melanogaster*, and found that their offspring showed quite a variety of new characteristics, which could also be found in very small numbers in a normal population. He found that the new characters bred true, showing that a true genetic change had occurred. Other experiments followed on a wide range of plants, insects and animals, and it was found that all types of nuclear radiations could produce mutations.[15]

It is reasonable to think of the mutation process as caused with a certain likelihood whenever the nuclear radiation passes through or near the genes. On this theory, which is only a simple picture of the complex processes actually occurring, the number of mutations must be directly proportional to the intensity of the nuclear radiation, however weak or strong it may be. There is no recovery after small doses. As far as it can be tested the proportionality between dose and genetic damage seems to hold, though it is impossible to test its validity for exceedingly small doses.

Genetic damage to man

Applying this knowledge to man, we can ascribe the presence in the population of certain deleterious genes to mutations occurring in the past. They could not have been present since the beginning of the human race, since in this case they would long ago have been eliminated by the reduced chance of survival they give to individuals carrying them. They are in fact constantly being eliminated for that reason, and so must be continually reappearing so that the total number is kept to the constant equilibrium value established over the centuries.

The causes of these continual mutations are many, but they certainly include the natural radiation to which we are all exposed. If they had all been due to this natural radiation, then doubling its intensity would double the number of mutations. In fact, since other causes operate, the effect would be considerably less than to double the natural rate. This

[15] H. J. Muller, "The Genetic Damage Produced by Radiation", *BAS*, *11*, 210 (1955); M. Westergaard, "Man's Responsibility to his Genetic Heritage", *BAS*, *11*, 318 (1955); H. J. Muller, "How Radiation Changes the Genetic Constitution", *BAS*, *11*, 329 (1955); J. F. Crow, "Genetic Effects of Radiation", *BAS*, *14*, 19 (1958).

rate of natural mutations, coupled with a knowledge of the intensity of the natural radiation, thus enables us to set a firm upper limit to the genetic damage that could be caused by radiation due to other sources. In this way it has been estimated that the dose required to double the natural mutation rate in man is about one rad per year. These figures are of importance in evaluating the genetic hazards due to nuclear explosions; this will be considered in Chapter V.

PERMISSIBLE RADIATION EXPOSURE

The whole problem of establishing permissible or tolerance doses of nuclear radiation is an exceedingly complex one. It has to be considered with regard to the somatic damage to the individual in his own lifetime and the genetic damage to his descendants. The number of people likely to be irradiated, whether it is a small occupational group or the whole population, has also to be taken into account.

Somatic damage

The tolerance dose for somatic damage can be bracketed between the natural dose and the smallest dose that has been known to cause observable injury. Over the years, the tolerance dose has been lowered several times as increasing knowledge brought new dangers to light. In 1928 it was 0·1 to 1 roentgen per day; in 1956 it was lowered to 0·1 roentgen per week.[16] These limits apply to people who deal professionally with nuclear radiations; the somatic danger to the population as a whole is very small, apart from those who are irradiated for medical reasons. Nowadays every person liable to come into contact with nuclear radiations carries a safety film which records how much radiation he has received. These are developed periodically, and if they show that an excessive dose has been received, the cause can be tracked down and eliminated, and appropriate medical treatment given.

[16] J. Schubert and R. E. Lapp, "Global Radiation Limits", *BAS, 14,* 23 (1958).

The somatic damage due to a given amount of radiation depends on the type of radiation, on whether it is delivered internally or externally and to what part of the body, and on the age and constitution of the person receiving it. It is likely that, with increasing knowledge, specific tolerance doses taking into account all these factors will be established. It will then become possible to use radiation of different types without either danger or undue caution in a wide variety of circumstances.[17]

Genetic damage

It is otherwise with the genetic effects. Although the effect of very small doses cannot be studied, all the evidence is consistent with there being no threshold for genetic damage, and this is supported by genetical theory. The damage is approximately proportional to the dose, however small or large it be. A tolerance dose cannot, therefore, be laid down for genetic damage. All that can be done is to establish approximately the probability of particular types of genetic damage in given sets of circumstances, and then it can be decided whether the risk is worth taking.[18]

The total genetic damage to a group of people depends on the intensity of the radiation to which they are exposed multiplied by the number of people in the group. The hazard thus depends very much on whether it is a small professional group or the whole population. Thus, for example, if a given exposure carried with it a chance in ten thousand of some

[17] W. F. Neuman, "The Somatic Effects of Fission Products", *BAS*, *14*, 15 (1958).

[18] T. C. Carter, "The Genetic Problem of Irradiated Human Populations", *BAS*, *11*, 362 (1955); "Radiation and Human Heredity", *BAS*, *11*, 364 (1955); P. Alexander, "Hazards of Atomic Radiation", *NS*, *4*, 622 (1958); W. R. Guild, "Biological Effects of Radiation", Ch. 5 of *Fall-Out* (Ed. J. M. Fowler), Basic Books, New York, 1960; "Radiation Hazards: British and U.S. Reports", *BAS*, *12*, 312 (1956); *The Effects of Atomic Radiation*, U.N. Scientific Committee, 1958; W. F. Neuman, "Uncertainties in Evaluating the Effects of Fall-out from Weapons Tests", *BAS*, *14*, 31 (1958).

genetic damage, this could perhaps be accepted for a group of ten people for a sufficiently serious reason, especially if they were above the normal reproductive age. But if a million people were involved, the number probably affected would be a hundred, and this is very serious indeed.[19]

Working along these lines, doses of radiation acceptable from the genetic point of view have been established. Typical levels of exposure are 5 rads per year for small professional groups of people, and the much smaller level of 0·1 rad per year for whole populations.

BENEFICIAL EFFECTS OF RADIATION

So far, all the biological effects of nuclear radiations mentioned have been harmful to man.[20] Sometimes, however, the damage they cause may be turned to good account. Nuclear radiations can destroy all living cells, especially those reproducing themselves, and this is very welcome when the growth is malignant and taking place at the expense of the rest of the organism. This happens in cancer, when groups of cells, for a reason not yet clearly understood, begin to multiply at an abnormally high rate, thus forming a tumour. This may grow rapidly, causing great pain and ultimately death. If, however, such a tumour is exposed to nuclear radiations its growth can be checked and even, in favourable cases, stopped entirely. By careful control of the irradiation it is possible to ensure that the malignant cells receive more radiation than the surrounding healthy cells, so they can be given a fatal dose while the healthy cells are unharmed. It is paradoxical that the same radiations that can induce cancer in a healthy cell will nevertheless destroy the malignant cell at a later date. Not all cancers can be treated by radiation, as some are

[19] S. H. Clark, "Genetic Radiation Exposures in the Field of Medicine", *BAS*, *12*, 14 (1956); K. Z. Morgan, "Human Exposure to Radiation", *BAS*, *15*, 384 (1959).

[20] This makes it possible to use them in war. See L. Ridenour, "How effective are Radioactive Poisons in Warfare?" *BAS*, *6*, 199 (1950).

too well established, but now there is an increasing chance of successful treatment providing it is begun in the early stages.

Medical uses of radiation

Many types of radiation can be used for this treatment. Until recently, the only rays available were those from radium. Radium needles, each containing a minute amount of radium, were frequently used. Now, electronic machines able to produce beams of penetrating nuclear radiation and radioactive isotopes are widely available, thus making it possible to treat much greater numbers of people than could ever be done with the very expensive radium.

The isotope cobalt 60 is particularly suitable for medical purposes, as it can easily be made by irradiating natural cobalt in a nuclear reactor, and emits gamma rays of the right energy. The rays are energetic enough to penetrate well into the body, but not so energetic that heavy and cumbersome shielding of the radioactive cobalt source is needed. For medical use, the isotope is encased in a massive lead box, from which the gamma rays can only escape by a narrow channel. The whole box, sometimes called a cobalt bomb, is so pivoted that the beam of gamma rays coming out of the channel can be directed at the patient at the required angle. Radioactive iridium 192 also finds medical application, as it has some advantages over cobalt 60 for particular purposes.[21]

Radioisotopes can also be used for medical diagnosis.[22] Many of the elements common in the body such as sodium and phosphorus have radioisotopes of convenient half-life.

[21] J. M. A. Lenihan, *Atomic Energy and its Applications*, p. 208, Pitman, London, 1954.
[22] E. E. Pochin, "Medical Uses of Atomic Energy", *ASJ*, *3*, 329 (1954); C. P. Rhoads, "The Medical Uses of Atomic Energy", *BAS*, *2*, 7–8, 22 (1946); R. H. Chamberlain, "Medical Use of Radiation", *BAS*, *14*, 39 (1958); M. D. Kamen, "Application of Isotopes to Biology", *BAS*, *1*, No. 12, 9 (1946); "Medical and Industrial Uses of Pile Products", *BAS*, *1*, No. 9, 1 (1946); *APD*, *3*, No. 1, 12 (1957); "Radioactive Isotopes in Medicine" (Ed. J. Rotblat), *NS*, *2*, No. 31, 29 (1957).

Wherever they go in the body they indicate their presence to suitable detecting instruments by the rays they continually emit. This is valuable for the study of metabolic processes. Thus if, for example, we want to know what the body does with the sodium in our food, then all that is necessary is to feed a patient with salt containing a very small amount of radioactive sodium called a "tracer". Then the sodium passes down through the body, enters the blood stream and is carried to the farthest extremities of the body, all the time emitting rays that show exactly where it has got to. The body treats the ordinary and the radioactive sodium in just the same way, so we learn how the body makes use of sodium in the form of salt. The detecting instruments are so sensitive that the amount of radioactive sodium needed is too small to cause any appreciable damage to the patient.

This is an extremely powerful way of studying the details of the metabolic processes taking place in the body, and one that is being increasingly used to advance our understanding of them. It has also been applied to study metabolic processes in animals and plants.

Genetic effects

Even the genetic effects of nuclear radiations can sometimes be turned to good account. Most of the mutations are changes for the worse, but very occasionally a new mutation is beneficial. It is in fact just through these rare beneficial mutations assisting the survival of the favoured individuals carrying them that species, including ourselves, have gradually evolved. The process of natural selection tends to weed out the many deleterious mutations and to preserve and multiply the beneficial ones.

In nature, this process of the perfection of species is a very long and gradual one, extending over perhaps millions of years. Survival of the fittest is an inefficient process that works in the long run but only at the expense of countless failures. Under human control, however, the process can be vastly accelerated, and new varieties produced, selected and crossed with each other in a very few generations.

Agricultural uses of radiation

The simplest method is just to expose a batch of seeds to nuclear radiations, and plant them out in the usual way. Many may have been killed by the exposure, but a very small proportion of improvements may have occurred. These can be selected from many millions of unsuccessful mutations and transferred to a specially favourable environment where they can reproduce many more of their kind. This research is still in its infancy, but it may well in the future be the source of improved varieties of plants and even of animals. Radioactive isotopes are also being extensively applied to control insect pests, and to prevent the deterioration of stored food.[23]

[23] R. S. Hannan, "Irradiation as a method of preserving food", NS, 15, 36 (1957).

CHAPTER IV

PEACEFUL APPLICATIONS

After the end of the war the urgency was removed from the work on the atomic bombs and many of the Los Alamos scientists returned to their university work. It became possible to think seriously about the possibility of utilizing the heat generated in the plutonium-producing reactors as a commercial source of power. The techniques for doing this were well known, as they were simply those used to generate electricity from coal in ordinary power stations. The only essential difference is that the nuclear fission reaction replaces burning coal as a source of heat. In both cases the heat is used to produce steam to drive a turbine that generates the electricity.

NUCLEAR POWER STATIONS

While the process was essentially understood, there remained the formidable metallurgical and engineering problems of actually building a nuclear power station. Furthermore, it was uncertain whether this way of producing electric power could compete economically with the existing methods. Despite these difficulties and doubts there was the continuing necessity of producing fissile material for military purposes to provide a powerful spur to intensive research on the different types of power-producing reactors. Furthermore, power is sometimes needed in circumstances where the cost is not the over-riding factor and nuclear power has very considerable advantages over all other power sources. An example of this is submarine propulsion. Nuclear power also held out the prospect of soon becoming economic in regions far from coal supplies where transport costs are the deciding factor.

Power resources

Although nuclear power is now more costly than coal power, it will certainly become progressively cheaper as time goes on, while the power from other sources will as certainly become gradually more and more expensive.[1] Nearly all our power is at present derived from energy given to the earth by the sun millions of years ago and now stored underground in the form of coal and oil. Known deposits are large but not unlimited. It has been estimated that, at the present rate of consumption, our oil will last for about 600 years and our coal for 5,000 years.[2] As time goes on, mining costs will rise, and the high-grade oils and coals will be rapidly exhausted.

Of the other sources of power, hydro-electric is important in mountainous countries, but still only accounts for seven per cent of the world's power. This fraction is unlikely to rise appreciably. Small contributions are made by wind power, natural gas, peat and wood. Although important locally, none of these is available in sufficient quantity to make a significant contribution to the power needs of the major industrial countries.

Surveys of available resources are inevitably uncertain because there are probably many coal and oil deposits still to be located. It is certain that world power needs will continue to increase, but it is difficult to be sure how rapidly they will do so. Estimates of how long coal and oil supplies will

[1] J. Marschak, "Economic Aspects of Atomic Power", BAS, 2, 5–6, 8 (1946). S. H. Schurr, "Economic Aspects of Atomic Energy as a Source of Power", BAS, 3, 117 (1947); S. H. Schurr, "Atomic Power in Selected Industries", BAS, 5, 301 (1949); J. E. Loftus, "Economic Aspects of Atomic Power", BAS, 7, 70 (1951).

[2] N. Lansdell, The Atom and the Energy Revolution, Penguin Books S.169, 1958; S. Devons, "World Power Resources", ASN, 1, 135 (1952); A. M. Weinberg, "Energy as an Ultimate Raw Material", Physics Today, 12, 18 (1959).

last vary, therefore, but there is general agreement that the situation will become increasingly difficult around the year 2000. A new source of power will be needed, and it is not too soon to begin developing it now.[3]

Extensive efforts have been made to improve existing power sources and to find new ones. Improved windmills have been designed, and solar heaters to make direct use of the sun's radiation.[4] Schemes are ready for harnessing the tides, and a cell has been perfected to burn hydrogen and oxygen so as to generate electricity directly. Some of these may well turn out to be useful for small-scale power generation, but at present none seems capable of making a significant contribution to world power needs.

Atomic power has thus become practicable at a time when a crisis due to the exhaustion of coal and oil is already in sight. This is the basic reason why every country able to do so has made great efforts in the field of atomic power.

The raw materials for atomic power are the uranium and thorium-bearing minerals. They are very widely spread over the earth's surface, and large deposits occur in the Congo, Czechoslovakia, the United States, Russia and Australia. Smaller deposits occur in practically every country, including France, South Africa, Sweden and Canada, though sometimes in such low concentrations that recovery is not economic.[5]

Pioneer work in Britain

Sustained efforts were made in Britain to develop atomic power from 1945 onwards.[6] Many of the British physicists

[3] Sir Harold Hartley, "Man's Use of Energy", *BAS*, *6*, 322 (1950).
[4] M. Telkes, "Future Uses of Solar Energy", *BAS*, *7*, 217 (1951).
[5] R. Nininger, "World Uranium Supplies", *BAS*, *15*, 249 (1959); C. F. Davidson, "World Uranium Supplies", *NS*, *14*, 9 (1957).
[6] K. E. B. Jay, *Britain's Atomic Factories*, H.M.S.O., London, 1954. Sir John Cockcroft, "Nuclear Power", *ASN*, *1*, 4 (1951); "The British Experimental Pile at Harwell", *ASN*, *1*, 36 (1951); "Nuclear Power", *ASN*, *1*, 281 (1952); F. E. Simon, "Prospects for Nuclear Power", *ASN*, *2*, 3 (1952); Sir Claude Gibb, "Industry and Atomic Power",

had worked with their American colleagues during the war
to develop the atomic bomb, and this included work on the
plutonium-producing reactors, essentially similar to the reactors that generate nuclear power. Yet, by the McMahon
Act of 1946,[7] the United States kept its scientific and technological knowhow secret in peacetime, even from those British
scientists who had unreservedly worked alongside them in
war. This secrecy was pushed to such extremes during the
McCarthy era that by the McCarran "Security" Act of 1950
some of these British scientists were even refused entry to the
United States to attend scientific meetings, a procedure that
American scientists were the first to condemn.[8]

The result of the McMahon Act was that while at the end
of the war the United States had large reactors already functioning, the British scientists had to start to build theirs
entirely from scratch, without even the benefit of the experience gained in the United States during wartime researches
to which they made so significant a contribution. A vast
industry had to be built at a time when Britain's economy
was trying to make the transition to peacetime production
and to repair the ravages of war.[9]

The centre for the fundamental scientific research was
established at Harwell on an old Royal Air Force aerodrome.
Under the direction of Sir John Cockcroft it soon began an

ASN, 2, 98 (1952); F. E. Simon, "Power from Atomic Energy", *ASJ*, 3,
247 (1954); P. Sporn, "Prospects in Industrial Application of Atomic
Energy", *BAS*, 6, 303 (1950).

[7] *BAS*, 1, No. 9; 2, Nos. 3–6 (1946).

[8] *ASN*, 1, 68 (1951); 2, 191 (1953); *ASJ*, 4, 59 (1954); "How to Lose
Friends", editorial in *BAS*, 8, 2 (1952); "A Protest against Visa
Situation", *BAS*, 8, 4 (1952); E. A. Shils, "America's Paper Curtain",
BAS, 8, 210 (1952); V. F. Weisskopf, "Report on The Visa Situation",
BAS, 8, 221 (1952); R. Aron, "American Visa Policy", *BAS*, 8, 234
(1952); "Whom We Shall Welcome", *BAS*, 9, 17 (1953); V. F. Weiss-
kopf, "Visas for Foreign Scientists", *BAS*, 10, 68 (1954); "American
Visa Policy", *BAS*, 11, 367 (1955); J. S. Toll, "Scientists Urge Lifting
Travel Restrictions", *BAS*, 14, 326 (1958).

[9] L. Bertin, *Atom Harvest*, Secker and Warburg, 1955.

extensive programme of work on the nuclear processes occurring in reactors and the nuclear and thermal properties of the materials used to build them. The engineers, led by Sir Christopher Hinton, plunged into the problems of building nuclear reactors, an entirely new field to them. A large factory was built at Capenhurst in Cumberland to separate U235 by the gaseous diffusion process, and two reactors to produce plutonium were constructed at Windscale.[10]

Initially, all this work was done by the Ministry of Supply. Later on, in 1954, responsibility for all military and industrial atomic research was transferred to a new body, the United Kingdom Atomic Energy Authority.

Calder Hall

After a very few years of intensive effort research had reached a sufficiently advanced stage for the first full-scale atomic power station to be designed and built at Calder Hall.[11] The first of the two reactors came into operation in April 1957, and the second not long after. Since that time they have almost continuously delivered 45 MW of power each to the National Electricity Grid. Four similar reactors are being built at Chapel Cross in Dumfriesshire.

Four groups of industrial companies were formed in the early 1950's to design and build atomic power stations for sale both in Britain and overseas. Each group is at present building one power station for the Central Electricity Authority. They are sited at Hinkley Point in Somerset (500 MW), at Berkeley in Gloucestershire (275 MW), at Bradwell in Essex (300 MW) and at Hunterston in Scotland

[10] K. E. B. Jay, *Britain's Atomic Factories*, H.M.S.O., 1954; H. W. B. Skinner, "Report to the U.S.A. on British Atomic Energy", *ASN*, 2, 350 (1953); Sir John Cockcroft, "The Application of Nuclear Energy to the Development of Useful Heat and Power", *ASN*, 2, 299 (1953); H. W. B. Skinner, "Britain's Nuclear Power Programme", *ASJ*, 4, 337 (1955); Sir Christopher Hinton, "Atomic Energy Developments in Great Britain", *ASJ*, 3, 264 (1954).

[11] K. Jay, *Calder Hall*, New York, Harcourt, Bruce and Co. London, Methuen, 1956.

(320 MW). Further stations are being planned for Dungeness (550 MW) and Trawsfynydd in North Wales (500 MW).[12]

All these reactors are graphite-moderated and gas-cooled. This design was chosen because it offered the best prospects of getting a reliable reactor working as soon as possible. There are many other designs possible, and research into their potentialities is being carried out at Harwell,[13] Aldermaston, Dounreay[14] in the north of Scotland and Winfrith Heath in Dorset.

Economics of nuclear power

It is a little difficult to calculate the cost of electricity generated by the nuclear power stations because they also produce plutonium, which is all purchased for use in nuclear weapons. They are designed to facilitate plutonium production, and the price paid for it is not determined by the ordinary processes of supply and demand, but is fixed by the U.K.A.E.A. However, if reasonable allowance is made for these uncertainties, Sir Christopher Hinton[15] has estimated that the cost of nuclear power will steadily fall from 0·67d. per kilowatt-hour in 1960 to 0·32d. in 1990. The cost of electricity from coal-fired power stations, on the other hand, is expected to remain at about 0·5d. per unit over the same period. Nuclear power is thus not economic in Britain at present, but it will probably become so in the 1970's.

Work in the United States

In the United States the abundance of oil makes power cheaper than in Britain, and so nuclear power cannot hope

[12] T. Margerison, "New Nuclear Power Stations", *NS, 6,* 10 (1957).

[13] "Report on the British Atomic Energy Research Establishment (Harwell)", *BAS, 7,* 229 (1951).

[14] Sir Christopher Hinton, "The Dounreay Fast Reactor", *NS, 6,* 1055 (1959).

[15] In a lecture in 1957. Also, *Nature, 187,* 1064 (1960).

to compete economically for many years.[16] There is, therefore, no particular hurry to construct a chain of full-scale power stations; it is best to spend the available effort on studying the characteristics of as many different types of reactors as possible. This has been done at many research centres, so that now the United States has operating experience of fast and slow reactors, heavy water reactors, and reactors cooled by liquid sodium or by carbon dioxide gas.[17] In addition there are whole ranges of reactors for special purposes including those to power submarines, aeroplanes, merchant ships and even earth satellites.

A full-scale power station (60 MW) has been built at Shippingport, and came into operation in December 1957.[18]

Other countries: Euratom

Many other countries have already built or are planning to build nuclear power stations. The first Russian installation (5 MW) came into operation in June 1954 and others are planned.[19] France,[20] Western Germany, Belgium, Holland, Norway, Sweden,[21] Switzerland, Japan and India have one or more research reactors and hope to build or import nuclear power stations. Six European countries are cooperating on atomic energy matters and pooling their resources.[22] On a larger scale, the International Atomic Energy Agency has

[16] S. H. Schurr and J. Marschak, *Economic Aspects of Atomic Power*, Princeton Univ. Press, 1950; O. A. Saunders, "Nuclear Power in Relation to Conventional Power Resources", *ASN, 2*, 11 (1952).

[17] R. F. Bacher, "The Development of Nuclear Reactors", *BAS, 5*, 80 (1949).

[18] *APD, 3*, No. 14, 3 (1958); No. 8, 2 (1957).

[19] A. M. Jonas, "Atomic Energy in Soviet Bloc Nations", *BAS, 15*, 379 (1959); A. Kramish, "Atomic Energy in the USSR", *BAS, 15*, 322 (1959).

[20] L. Kowarski, "Atomic Energy Developments in France", *BAS, 4*, 139 (1948); F. Perrin, "Atomic Energy in France", *BAS, 11*, 92 (1955).

[21] H. Lundbergh, "Sweden's Atomic Energy Program", *BAS, 15*, 219 (1959).

[22] E. Hirsch, "A Guide to Euratom", *BAS, 15*, 250 (1959); Sir Harold Hartley, "Target for Euratom", *NS, 2*, 27, 35 (1957).

been established to accelerate the peaceful uses of atomic energy throughout the world,[23] and periodical U.N. Conferences assist the dissemination of new knowledge.[24]

There are, however, many difficult problems to be solved before nuclear reactors can supply the bulk of the world's power. At present, there is no reactor that is both safe and economic to run. Safe reactors can be built of fully enriched fuel but they are not economic. Economic reactors can be built using natural uranium, but they are not safe for industrial areas.

Underdeveloped areas

There are great possibilities in the use of atomic power stations to open up remote regions. They could pump water from great distances in situations where coal-fired power stations would be quite uneconomic, and supply power for the processing of minerals. Unfortunately, however, the countries that are most in need of such developments are usually quite unable to pay the substantial cost, in the region of £50M or $140M, of such power stations. Indeed, it is likely that the poorer countries have sometimes tended to place too much emphasis on atomic power to solve their problems, to the detriment of the more immediately needed development in the biological and medical sciences.[25]

NUCLEAR PROPULSION

In addition to their use as generators of electricity, nuclear reactors can also be used for propulsion.[26] There are two serious limitations to this: they are very heavy and their cores are highly radioactive. Generally speaking, the larger and

[23] APD, Special Supplement, 1957; BAS, 15, 160 (1959); B. B. Bechhoefer, BAS, 14, 147 (1958).

[24] BAS, 15, 18 (1959); ASJ, 5, 73 (1955).

[25] S. Dedijer, "The Birth and Death of a Myth", BAS, 14, 164 (1958); M. J. Deutch, "Can We Afford Atomic Power for Underdeveloped Countries?" BAS, 16, 23 (1960).

[26] "Nuclear Energy for Transport", NS, No. 23, 25 (1957).

heavier reactors weighing hundreds of tons are more efficient as sources of power than the smaller ones, and even these may weigh fifty to a hundred tons. It is, therefore, economical to generate the power as electricity in large stationary reactors and use it to drive the means of transport. This can be done in the case of trains, for example, but not for ships and aeroplanes. The second limitation, that due to the radioactive core, means that there must be no possibility that the reactor could be broken open and its contents scattered due to an accidental collision. This consideration is of particular importance for aeroplanes. Over and above these two limitations is the economic question of whether nuclear propulsion is cheaper than what is used already.

Merchant ships and submarines

These factors combine to make ship propulsion the first candidate for nuclear power. The engines of ships already weigh many hundreds of tons and their replacement by reactors of corresponding power presents few fundamental difficulties. Like land-based reactors, the heat they develop is used to generate high-pressure steam, which can be used directly to drive the turbines connected to the propeller shafts. The reactor must be heavily shielded to prevent radiations from its core reaching the cargo or crew, but the weight of the shields required is not prohibitive. A counterbalancing factor to the weight of a ship reactor and the space it occupies is that there is no need to make provision for storage of bulky fuels, as the fuel for very many journeys is contained within the reactor itself. The reactor and shield can be so massively constructed that there is little danger of radioactive contamination in the event of a collision.

The technological difficulties of designing a nuclear marine propulsion unit have essentially been solved, but their cost is still many times that of the coal- and oil-fired marine engines already in use. This is why the first nuclear-driven ships were the submarines *Nautilus* and *Skate* built in the

United States.[27] Here the economic considerations take second place to the need for prolonged underwater operation without refuelling. A whole range of nuclear-powered naval ships, up to aircraft carriers, is now being built in the United States, together with the nuclear merchant ship *Savannah*.[28] In Russia a nuclear ice-breaker, the *Lenin*, was launched in December 1957.[29]

If the economics of driving merchant ships by nuclear power is examined, it is found that it is very much more expensive for existing merchant ships than coal or oil power. So, although some nuclear ships may be built for demonstration purposes, they are unlikely to be built as commercial propositions. However, if our preconceived ideas about ships are set aside and the whole problem of driving ships by nuclear power considered afresh, it is found that the larger the ship the more economical it becomes to use nuclear power to drive it. So it is likely that the merchant ships of the future will be large vessels of 100,000 tons and more, driven at speeds considerably higher than are usual today by nuclear engines of immense power. It may quite possibly be advantageous to run them fifty to a hundred feet below the surface to avoid storms. Large passenger ships may well be driven by nuclear power, but at present their economics are borderline, especially in view of the competition from the air. Smaller passenger ships of the future are unlikely to be driven by nuclear power.

Trains

Nuclear-powered trains are already being seriously studied, though they are not nearly such an attractive proposition as

[27] E. E. Kintner, "Machinery for the Nautilus", *NS*, *5*, 694 (1959); *BAS*, *14*, 193 (1958); *APD*, *3*, No. 14, 8 (1958); No. 5, 8 (1957); No. 13, 8 (1958).

[28] *Nature*, *184*, 677 (1959); "Development of a Nuclear-Powered Merchant Ship", *BAS*, *11*, 229 (1955); A. C. Harcy, "Nuclear Merchant Ships", *NS*, *4*, 1219 (1958).

[29] J. Bremmer, "Russia's Nuclear-Powered Icebreaker", *NS*, *6*, 499 (1959).

ships.[30] They need to be very heavy and powerful if they are to be economically practicable, and the danger of collision and release of radioactivity is much more serious than for ships because of their higher speeds and less massive construction. It is obviously much better to run the trains by electricity generated by a stationary reactor. This is already being done, though the trains are exactly the same as electric trains driven by an ordinary power station and it would be a misnomer to speak of them as nuclear trains. Electric trains run in this way are practicable when the railway is never very far from the nearest power station, as is the case over most of Europe. However, in other parts of the world, the United States or Russia for example, trains run for many thousands of miles over inhospitable terrain. Such lines would be extremely costly to electrify, and it may well be that nuclear engines would be an economic proposition for them. The engines used on such journeys have to be very powerful, which favours nuclear propulsion, large quantities of fuel would no longer have to be carried on the journey, and the consequences of a collision would be less serious than in a populated area.

Motor-cars

The same reasons that make nuclear railway engines unlikely apply with much greater force to motor-cars. The weight, cost and collision factors are each sufficient to rule out nuclear motor-cars. However, cars can in principle be driven by electricity stored in batteries that are replenished from the mains between journeys. This method is already used for milk delivery carts and other small vehicles, but with the present batteries not enough energy can be stored for efficient use in motor-cars. But if a light, efficient way of storing electrical energy is developed this could well be the basis of the car of the future. Cheaper electricity from nuclear power stations could make the cost compete with petrol, to

[30] *BAS, 10,* 142 (1954).

say nothing of the saving due to the absence of both noise and exhaust fumes.

Aeroplanes

Aeroplanes driven by nuclear power are even more unattractive than trains. The economic factors are perhaps not so severe, but the weight of reactors, and the catastrophic consequences of a crash, make the nuclear aeroplane a very difficult proposition. There is no fundamental reason why they should not work, however, and considerable research is being done on them.[31] In principle they are delightfully simple, consisting of just a nuclear reactor with tubes running through it from the front to the back, like a ramjet engine. The reactor heats the air drawn in, and it expands and rushes out at the rear, driving the plane forward like an ordinary jet engine. This process would only begin to operate at a certain speed, so the initial acceleration would be done by conventional means. It is likely that nuclear-powered planes will ultimately fly, but it seems unlikely that they will replace those powered by petrol and jet engines.[32]

HARNESSING NUCLEAR FUSION

All these considerations concerning nuclear propulsion will need revision if the fusion reactor proves feasible. The cost and weight of fusion reactors will be comparable with that of fission reactors, but the danger of radioactive contamination in the event of an accident is very much less. This removes one of the serious difficulties, but the others remain, so it is unlikely that fusion reactors will much modify the picture in this century, though it is always possible that some quite new approach will be found.

All the peaceful applications of atomic energy described

[31] L. R. Hafstad, "Atomic Power for Aircraft", *BAS, 5,* 309 (1949).
[32] A. V. Cleaver, "Nuclear Energy and Rocket Propulsion in Aeronautics", *ASN, 2,* 293 (1953).

so far derive their energy from the fission process. This is not the only way of getting energy from the nucleus; as has been seen already, energy is also released when very light nuclei fuse together. This is the basic process of the hydrogen bomb. Is it possible to tame the hydrogen bomb so that its energy also is made available for peaceful purposes?

Controlling the fusion reaction

The fusion reaction begins when a mass of light nuclear material is raised to such a high temperature that the individual nuclei can overcome their natural coulomb repulsion when colliding, and coalesce to form heavier nuclei. The reaction becomes self-propagating as soon as the heat generated in the fusion reactions exceeds the heat lost through radiation and other causes. This state is reached when the reacting mass is at a very high temperature, some millions of degrees, and thereafter the reaction goes with explosive violence. In the case of the fission reaction, the process can be easily controlled because the whole mass of uranium does not have to be heated, and the delayed neutrons enable the reaction to be damped down at will. Neither of these conditions holds for fusion reactions; they are very fast and very hot, so hot that any container that could be made would be instantly vaporized by them.

It is clearly no easy matter to control a fusion reaction, but at the present time immense scientific effort is being spent on the problem because of the potential advantages of fusion power.[33]

Need for fusion power

Fusion power is needed because fission power cannot last for ever. There is only a limited amount of fissile material present in the earth's crust, and as the more easily mined

[33] T. Margerison, "Power from Nuclear Fusion?" *NS*, *10*, 35 (1957); A. E. Robson, "Alternative Roads to Thermonuclear Power", *NS*, *4*, 657 (1958); W. P. Allis, *Nuclear Fusion*, Van Nostrand, 1960; D. Curry and B. R. Newman, *The Challenge of Fusion*, Van Nostrand, 1960.

deposits are exhausted, the price of the raw material will steadily rise. There is no immediate worry, as known deposits are sufficient to meet world power needs for about a hundred million years, but in the end it will be exhausted. Quite apart from this, fission power has several disadvantages, the most notable being the inevitable accumulation of highly radioactive fission products. At present these can be used in many industrial and other processes, and the rest disposed of with some difficulty. But if a major part of the world's power supply is derived from fission the fission products will accumulate at a rate far exceeding all conceivable uses, and it will be an increasingly serious problem to know what to do with them.[34]

Advantages of fusion power

Fusion power suffers from neither of these disadvantages. It has no long-lived radioactive products to cause disposal problems. The raw material can be deuterium, which occurs in the proportion of one in 5,000 in ordinary water. Deuterium can be extracted from sea-water at a cost of a few shillings per gram. If this deuterium is burnt by the fusion process it would give the same amount of energy as five or ten tons of coal. One ton of deuterium is thus equivalent to about three million tons of coal. Put another way, a gallon of sea-water contains in its deuterium the same energy as a hundred gallons of petrol.[35]

It can be estimated that there are about a million million million tons of water in the sea, and this contains deuterium equivalent to about sixty times this weight of coal. If the energy was used at the rate of six thousand million tons of coal a year, equivalent to four times the present world power

[34] W. De Laguna, "What is Safe Waste Disposal?" *BAS*, *15*, 35 (1959); J. G. Terrill, "Some Public Health Aspects of Radioactive Wastes", *BAS*, *14*, 44 (1958).

[35] T. Margerison, "Can We get Power from Nuclear Fusion?" *NS*, *10*, 35 (1957).

consumption, it would last ten thousand million years. Thus even if it were possible to use only a small fraction of the available deuterium, it would supply all conceivable power needs for an unimaginably long time: long before it is exhausted man will have solved the problem of interplanetary and probably interstellar travel, and will be able without difficulty to find somewhere else to live. On a less speculative level, even a relatively inefficient method of tapping the energy in deuterium could revolutionize world power supplies, with all that this would imply in the reduced cost of transport and all manufacturing processes.

The research programme

This is the vision that inspires the arduous and expensive researches on the problem of attaining an economic controlled thermonuclear reaction. The projected research programme can be divided into four stages. First of all it is necessary to build an experimental apparatus in which a fusion reaction can be shown to be taking place. Then it has to be improved so that the reaction goes on long enough for appreciable amounts of power to be produced. The next stage is to increase the power output to the level where more power is being produced than is used to heat the material to fusion temperatures in the first place. Finally, when all this has been done, an economically sound fusion power station must be designed and built. Even then, the project will still be in its infancy, as a long series of developments and modifications will be needed before the fusion power stations attain their most efficient form.

Since the heat of the sun and the stars is derived from thermonuclear reactions, mainly by the linked series of nuclear reactions called the hydrogen cycle and the carbon cycle,[36] it

[36] H. A. Bethe, "Energy Production in Stars", *Physical Review*, 55, 434 (1939); H. Bondi and E. E. Salpeter, "Thermonuclear Reactions and Astrophysics", *Nature*, 169, 304 (1952); E. E. Salpeter, "Energy Production in Stars", *Annual Review of Nuclear Science, 2*, 41 (1953); R. E. Marshak, "The Energy of Stars", *Scientific American, 182*, 1, 42 (1950).

might be thought that the best approach to controlled fusion power would be to try to reproduce these reactions on earth. Unfortunately, however, these will only work in an immense mass of material which acts as a stabilizer. Their energy release per unit mass is remarkably small, less than one hundredth of that in the human body, but the mass of the sun is so large that this small energy release is sufficient to keep the sun at its high temperature, pouring energy out in all directions at a rate equivalent to burning four million tons of matter a second. The smallness of the energy release per unit mass, however, makes the reaction quite unsuitable for a terrestrial power station, even if it had not been ruled out for other reasons. The faster deuterium reactions must be used instead, and this leads to the acute problem of containing the reacting material so that the reaction neither dies down nor becomes explosive.

Plasmas

At present the research is concentrated on the first stage. A number of experiments are being made, both in Britain and abroad, to produce a thermonuclear reaction.[37] At fusion temperatures all material is vaporized, and most of the electrons are stripped from their nuclei. Matter in this state is called a plasma. Due to their high temperature, plasmas exert a very high pressure outwards, and also lose energy rapidly by radiation. Both these processes cool the plasma and thus stop the fusion reaction. The main research effort is thus directed to the problem of producing a plasma and then

[37] R. F. Post, "Controlled Fusion Research. An Application of the Physics of High Temperature Plasmas", *Reviews of Modern Physics*, *28*, 338 (1956); J. D. Lunz, "From Perhapsatron to Columbus", *Nucleonics, 13,* 23 (1955); A. Simon, *An Introduction to Thermonuclear Research*, Pergamon, 1959; *Controlled Nuclear Fusion*, Vols. 31 and 32 of the *Proceedings of the Second International Conference on the Peaceful Uses of Atomic Energy* (Geneva, September, 1958); R. F. Post, "Fusion Power", *Scientific American*, December, 1957; L. Spitzer, "The Stellarator", *Scientific American*, October, 1958.

restraining it in a small volume for long enough for the fusion reaction to take place.

The fireball of an atomic bomb is an example of a plasma, but it is no use producing it in this way for fusion research. Another way of making a plasma is by passing a very high-voltage electric discharge through a tube of gas. The high current strips the electrons off the gas atoms and raises the whole to a high temperature, thus forming a plasma. It was noticed that this plasma first filled the whole tube and then, impelled by its inherent electromagnetic forces, contracted rapidly towards the axis of the tube. This was discovered as early as 1932 by Tonks and is known as the pinch effect. The plasma soon expands again, but at the moment of greatest contraction its temperature can attain very high values, approaching those required for a fusion reaction.

Sceptre and Zeta

It was soon found that the very high currents tended to corrode the electrodes that were in contact with the plasma. This difficulty was overcome by bending the tube round into a circle so that it formed a doughnut or toroidal shape. The electric discharge can be induced in such a toroidal volume of gas by passing an electric current through a wire wound round the toroid on the same principle as the transformer. The plasma then contracts to the axial ring and is never in contact with any electrodes. This is the principle behind the Sceptre machines built by Dr A. A. Ware under the direction of Sir George Thomson at Imperial College, London, and subsequently moved to the A.E.I. laboratories at Aldermaston, the Zeta machine built by Dr Thonemann and colleagues at Harwell, and many similar machines in the United States and the U.S.S.R.[38]

[38] L. S. Artsimovich, "Research on Controlled Thermonuclear Reactions in the U.S.S.R.", *Soviet Physics* (*Uspekhi*), *66*, 191 (1958); I. V. Kurchatov, "The Possibility of Producing Thermonuclear Reactions in a Gas Discharge", *ASJ*, *5*, 375 (1956); I. Kurchatov, "Controlled Thermonuclear Reactions", *BAS*, *12*, 269 (1956); M. B.

Very high temperatures, approaching a million degrees, were obtained with the early versions of these machines, but they did not last long as the electric discharge turned out to be extremely unstable. The circular ring of induced, pinched discharge wriggled violently and hit the walls in less than a millionth of a second. These instabilities are being controlled by imposing an axial magnetic field on the discharge; this is equivalent to containing the plasma in a magnetic bottle. Since a plasma consists wholly of charged particles, it is very responsive to applied electric or magnetic fields, and this makes containment a possibility. Several ingenious arrangements of electromagnetic fields to contain the plasma are being studied. The charged particles are forced into tight spiral orbits around the field lines, and are prevented from escaping by a magnetic mirror, formed when the field strength increases.

Even if this containment problem is solved, and a thermonuclear reaction established in the plasma, there still remains the formidable problems of extracting the heat from the plasma and making the whole process economic. It may prove possible to extract the energy directly from the plasma as electricity without the intervening heat exchangers, boilers, steam turbines and generators that increase the capital cost and reduce the efficiency of existing fission power stations. All this lies in the future, and a great deal of difficult scientific and engineering research will be necessary before success is achieved. The problems to be solved are more formidable than was at first thought, and it is clear that a much deeper understanding of the behaviour of plasmas will have to be

Gottlieb, "The Stellarator and other Thermonuclear Projects in the United States", *Endeavour, 19,* 62 (1960); *Proceedings of the Second United Nations International Conference on the Peaceful Uses of Atomic Energy,* Volumes 31 and 32 (United Nations, Geneva, 1958); J. B. Adams, *Fusion Problems* (CERN, Geneva. 59–61); *Fisica del Plasma: Esperimenti e Techniche,* Italian Physical Society Conference, N. Zanichelli, Bologna, 1960; S. Glasstone and R. H. Lovberg, *Controlled Thermonuclear Reactions,* Van Nostrand, 1960.

gained before further advances can be made. In spite of the difficulties, many scientists are optimistic that they will ultimately be overcome.

A near miss: muon catalysis

It is possible that an entirely new approach might solve the problem of utilizing fusion reactions. An interesting possibility, that only just failed, followed from the discovery that muons can assist nuclei to fuse together.[39] Muons are unstable charged particles of mass about 207 times that of the electron. They can combine with protons in the same way as electrons do to form a mesonic hydrogen atom. This is just the same as an ordinary hydrogen atom, except that it has a muon in place of its electron in an orbit 207 times closer to the proton, because of the greater muonic mass. Such a hydrogen atom is electrically neutral, and can, therefore, approach very close to any other light nucleus like that of deuterium, and this helps them to fuse. There is no need to heat up the deuterium as in the case of a thermonuclear reaction. If fusion takes place, the muon is liberated, and is available to catalyse further fusions. This might have been a practicable way to fuse atoms on a large scale, as muons are not too difficult to produce. Unfortunately, however, muons are unstable, having an average life of about two-millionths of a second, and so they break up before they have catalysed enough fusions to make the process worth while. This method is therefore not a practicable proposition, but it was a near enough miss to show that there may yet be a surprise solution to the fusion problem.

Peaceful nuclear explosions

There has been some discussion of the possibility of using atomic explosives to assist in mining and blasting operations.

[39] J. W. Jackson, "Catalysis of Nuclear Reactions between Hydrogen Isotopes by Muons", *Physical Review, 106,* 330 (1957); R. E. Peierls, "A New Way to Fuse Atoms", *NS, 7,* 36 (1957); N. D'Angelo, "Mesons and the Catalysis of Nuclear Reactions", *American Journal of Physics, 27,* 466 (1959).

The radioactive hazard would seem to make this unattractive, except perhaps for limited use in regions remote from centres of population.[40]

INDUSTRIAL USES OF RADIOACTIVE ISOTOPES

Atomic energy has other industrial applications apart from its use as a source of power. Radioactive isotopes are finding a multitude of applications due to the special properties of the radiations they emit.[41] These include their ability to ionize the air and to penetrate considerable thicknesses of solid material.

The ionizing power can be put to good use whenever it becomes necessary to make the air more conductive than usual. For example, in cotton spinning the motion of the thread can lead to large accumulations of static electricity, particularly on a dry day. These could become so large that sparking takes place, with consequent danger of fire. Now, a radioactive isotope can be placed near the looms to render the air conducting so that the charge leaks away gradually before any harm is done.

The penetrating power of the radiations from isotopes leads to more applications. In many continuous processes, such as making paper or steel strip, it is important to keep a close check on the thickness of the product. Previously, this

[40] F. Reines, "The Peaceful Nuclear Explosion", *BAS*, *15*, 118 (1959); "Are there Peaceful Engineering Uses of Atomic Explosives?" *BAS*, *6*, 171 (1950); W. F. Libby, "Nuclear Energy—Some New Aspects", *BAS*, *15*, 240 (1959); T. F. Gaskell, "Underground Atomic Bombs to Free Oil?" *NS*, 5, 113, 115 (1959); G. W. Johnson, "Peaceful Nuclear Explosions—Status and Promise", *Nucleonics*, *18*, 49 (1960).

[41] G. N. Walton, "The Utilisation of Fission Products", *ASJ*, *3*, 200 (1954); P. Aebersold, "Isotopes and their Application to Peacetime Uses of Atomic Energy", *BAS*, *4*, 151 (1948); T. K. Glennan, "New Horizons for Industry in the Isotopes Field", *BAS*, *7*, 174 (1951); J. K. Dawson, "Fission Fragments in the Chemical Industry", *NS*, *5*, No. 111, 31 (1959); S. Jefferson, "Uses for Spent Fuel", *NS*, *15*, 33 (1957); H. M. Finniston, "Peaceful Plutonium", *NS*, *5*, 9, 181 (1959).

could only be done by stopping at intervals to measure the thickness with a micrometer. Now all that has to be done is to put a suitable isotope on one side of the strip and a detector on the other. Since the rays are gradually absorbed by the matter they pass through, any variation in the thickness of the strip will be reflected by a variation in the reading of the detector. Thus a continuous check can be kept on the thickness without the necessity of stopping the machine. So simple a device as this can lead to the saving of many thousands of pounds every year.

Radioactive counters can be used to count the numbers of some product passing along a conveyor belt. A beam of nuclear radiations can be arranged to pass from source to detector across the path of the moving product. A recorder can register each time the beam is interrupted, and hence the number of products passing along the belt.

Such simple applications as these are already estimated to be saving industry in the United States over $500M per year (1957), and it is likely that there are many more applications still to be found and developed.

CHAPTER V

NUCLEAR EXPLOSIONS

When a chain reaction is established in a mass of fissile material, either by bringing together two sub-critical masses or by implosion, an immense amount of energy is released in a very small volume. The reacting mass is instantly vaporized and raised to a temperature of several millions of degrees, and expands with explosive violence. As soon as this happens the chain reaction ceases, but so short is the time taken from the emission of a neutron from one nucleus undergoing fission to its capture by the next fissile nucleus that about seventy generations of the chain reaction can take place in the millionth of a second that the reacting mass remains together.

Since each generation roughly doubles the energy release, the last few generations are all-important. No container would be strong enough to keep the reacting mass together because of the intense heat and enormous pressure developed, but the expansion can be delayed by a tenth of a microsecond by surrounding the uranium with a heavy material like tungsten. The sheer inertia of the tungsten tamper keeps the reaction going for the few vital extra millimicroseconds.

PHYSICAL EFFECTS

The fireball and mushroom

When the tamper has been brushed aside, the incandescent ball of gas expands out to a distance of several hundred feet. This fireball consumes everything in its path, and any combustible material it touches is reduced immediately to ashes.

The fireball is intensely radioactive, since it contains all the fission fragments from the uranium as well as the neutrons left over when the reaction comes to an end. These neutrons can themselves enter surrounding nuclei in the air and on the ground, frequently rendering them radioactive as well.

The outward momentum of the expanding fireball is gradually spent, leaving a vast bubble of hot, radioactive gas. This bubble, now lighter than the surrounding air, rises rapidly to a great height, carrying with it most of the fission fragments and the dust of pulverized buildings. As it rises, the bubble expands and spreads out, the water vapour condenses into cloud, and the familiar mushroom is formed.

The heat flash

Far below on the ground, a complex series of events has already taken place. From the first few instants of the nuclear reaction, an intensely powerful burst of radiation is emitted from the fireball. To the observer, this appears as a brilliant flash, so bright that anyone looking directly towards it from as near as a few miles away would be permanently blinded. The observers of the first test, though they were facing away from the explosion and wearing the darkest glasses, were dazzled by it. The flash is powerful enough to ignite paper and wood up to a distance of about a mile, and can cause severe burns on exposed skin out to considerably greater distances.

To give a more precise idea of the effects of this heat flash the power of the bomb must be specified. The intensity of the heat flash varies as the square root of the distance from the point of explosion, while that of the blast wave (to be described below) varies roughly as the cube root of the power of the bomb. This is because the radiation does not greatly affect the air through which it passes, and so is a surface effect attenuated according to the inverse square law, while the blast wave affects the whole volume through which it passes and so is attenuated according to an inverse cube law.

A consequence of this is that the heat flash is proportionately more important than the blast wave for large explosions, while the blast wave dominates in the smaller explosions. In ordinary high-explosive bombs, for example, the blast wave does all the damage, and the effect of the flash is negligible. For atomic bombs the blast wave is still more important than the flash. For hydrogen bombs, however, the heat flash might well prove even more destructive than the blast wave. It is therefore more realistic, in discussing the effect of the heat flash, to do so with reference to a typical hydrogen bomb.

If we take the power of such a bomb to be ten megatons, then fairly precise estimates can be given of the damage due to the heat flash at different distances from the point of explosion. Assuming good visibility, the flash itself will be seen over a very wide area, even in broad daylight. At a distance of fourteen miles, about three calories (a unit of heat) will reach each square centimetre of exposed surface. This is sufficient to scorch dark paper and cause first-degree burns on exposed skin. At twelve miles second-degree burns will be produced and there is danger of forest fires in dry weather. Coming farther in, about fifteen calories per square centimetre will be delivered at a distance of ten miles, and this can ignite white paper, curtains and wood, and cause severe third-degree burns. Nearer than about eight miles, the irradiation rises to thirty or forty calories per square centimetre, and this is sufficient to ignite instantly all combustible material in its path.

For bombs of other sizes, the corresponding effects can easily be estimated by scaling the distances according to the square root of the power. Thus, for a bomb of forty megatons, all the distances given above should be doubled. Bombs of this size are quite conceivable; one of the early test explosions had a power in the region of fifteen megatons.[1]

The heat flash, being essentially electromagnetic radiation,

[1] This is equivalent to about eleven times the total weight of explosives dropped on Germany during the last war, and to about eighty times that dropped by the Germans on Great Britain.

travels outward from the explosion with the speed of light. There is thus no chance of taking shelter; the damage is done before anyone has any opportunity to react.

The blast wave

It is otherwise with the blast or shock wave caused by the immense pressure created in the fireball. This pressure wave travels outwards at roughly the speed of sound, or 700 m.p.h. A person ten miles from the explosion has nearly a minute to seek shelter in the interval between seeing the flash and the arrival of the blast wave. This is long enough to get downstairs and into a shelter.

When the blast wave arrives, there is a rapid increase in pressure. It falls quite rapidly and is followed by a longer period of reduced pressure. The effect on anything in its path is thus a sharp push followed by a longer suction. If a bomb of ten megatons is again taken as standard for purposes of comparison, then the blast overpressure at a distance of twenty miles is about one pound per square inch (psi), which is sufficient to shatter all windows and damage plaster and window frames. At fourteen miles the overpressure is 2 psi, which can cause some structural distortion of wooden houses, blow doors in, and cause considerable plaster damage. At twelve miles, window frames are blown in with severe plaster damage and twenty-five per cent danger of non-fatal injuries.

So far the damage is not catastrophic. Though considerable inconvenience is caused, the damage is repairable, and houses can be lived in while the repairs are being made. At distances less than ten miles, however, the damage becomes more serious. The overpressure at ten miles is about 4 psi, and this will destroy most wooden frame buildings and cause ten per cent fatal and thirty per cent non-fatal injuries. At eight miles, there is severe structural damage to steel frame buildings, and 9-inch brick walls are cracked. At six miles and nearer most large trees are broken off or blown over, 12-inch brick walls severely cracked, and smaller brick buildings reduced to rubble.[2]

Here again, the effects of bombs of different power may be estimated by scaling the above distances according to the cube root of the power of the bomb. There is no convincing evidence that the explosion of nuclear bombs has any significant effect on the world's weather.[3]

RADIOACTIVE EFFECTS

These two types of damage, due to the heat flash and the blast wave, are already familiar as the effects of ordinary high-explosive bombs. The other effects of nuclear weapons, due to their radioactive properties, have no such familiar counterparts. They are the direct effects of the radiation emitted during the explosion and of the fall-out of radioactive dust that is scattered over a wide area.

Direct radiation

The direct nuclear radiation consists of gamma rays accompanying the heat flash, and high-energy particles, mostly neutrons and electrons, emitted from the fission fragments and from the surrounding material made radioactive by the explosion. These are not very penetrating, and cause little damage over and above that due to the heat flash and the blast wave. If the explosion takes place on or near the ground, however, a considerable amount of residual radio-

[2] This information is derived principally from the article "South Woodley looks at the H-bomb", by H. A. Knapp, *BAS, 10,* 306 (1954); *ASJ, 4,* 261 (1955). For further accounts on the effects of nuclear weapons, see "Nuclear Weapons" (*Manual of Civil Defence,* Vol. 1, Pamphlet No. 1, H.M.S.O., 1956); *The Effects of the Atomic Bombs at Hiroshima and Nagasaki,* by the British Mission to Japan (H.M.S.O., 1946); *The Effects of Atomic Weapons* (McGraw-Hill, 1950); *ASN, 4,* 36 (1950); J. O. Hirschfelder, "The Effects of Atomic Weapons", *BAS, 6,* 236 (1950); *Nuclear Explosions and their Effects* (Government of India, 1956); Sir Geoffrey Taylor, "The formation of a blast wave by a very intense explosion", *Proc. Roy. Soc.* 201*A,* 159, 1950.

[3] Sir Graham Sutton, "Thermonuclear Explosions and the Weather", *Nature, 175,* 319 (1955).

activity may remain to contaminate the area around the explosion centre.

Fall-out

The greatest danger due to radioactivity comes from the fall-out, especially from the large "three-decker" hydrogen bombs. The debris from the explosion, consisting principally of fission fragments and radioactive dust, is carried high into the air by the fireball, and dispersed by the prevailing winds.[4] The heavier particles fall back to earth within a few days, and may heavily contaminate a cigar-shaped area extending for hundreds of miles in the direction down-wind from the explosion. If the bomb is a large one, and derives most of its energy from fission, this contamination can be very serious indeed. Thus, it was estimated that the 1954 Pacific test contaminated an area of several thousand square miles with enough fall-out to give a lethal dose to anyone living in the area.

This hazard is primarily a somatic one; the people exposed to this immediate fall-out suffer radiation sickness from which most of them eventually recover. This was the experience of the crew of the *Lucky Dragon* and of the several hundred Marshall Islanders who were affected by the Bikini test.

The contamination can find its way to the human body in several ways. The dust can be directly inhaled and absorbed by the body. Most of this soon passes through but some may be retained, especially strontium 90, a metal chemically similar to calcium.

The radioactive dust can also collect on the clothes and in the interior of houses, eventually coming into contact with the skin. This hazard is not so serious because most of the dangerous radiation is absorbed by the dead outer layers of the skin. Dust falling on growing crops and vegetables can

[4] L. Machta and R. T. List, *Fall-Out* (Ed. J. M. Fowler), Basic Books, New York, 1960, Ch. 2.

also find its way to the human body either directly or via milk or animal flesh.

The smaller fragments of radioactive debris may be carried right round the earth by the winds high in the stratosphere. It may take many years for the smallest particles to reach the earth's surface, so these are spread rather unevenly over the whole earth. The distribution depends partly on the prevailing winds and partly on the weather conditions. Rain tends to bring down any dust particles with it, and so areas of high rainfall receive more than the average amount of radioactivity. It has proved possible to detect the increased radioactivity of rainfall a few days after a nuclear explosion at distances of thousands of miles.

The hazard due to this radioactivity depends on the extent to which the rain is retained in the soil. If the soil lacks an element and the same element or a similar element occurs among the fission products, then it tends to be preferentially retained. For example, strontium tends to be retained in regions with soil of low calcium content. Again, some animals and plants are able to accumulate certain elements, and some have been found to have collected remarkable amounts of radioactivity. This could easily be an unexpected hazard if the plant or animal were used for food.

Strontium 90

The radioactive fission fragments consist of a mixture of a large number of types of nuclei. The hazard due to a particular isotope depends on its half-life and on the biological effectiveness of the radiation it emits. If the half-life is very short, in the region of seconds to days, most of the radioactivity will decay before it comes into contact with human beings. On the other hand, if the half-life is very long, in the region of thousands of years, then the number of nuclei decaying per unit time is very small. Thus the short-lived and long-lived isotopes constitute little hazard, while those of medium half-lives are the most dangerous. Among these is strontium 90, which has a half-life of about twenty-eight years, and emits 0·6 MeV beta rays, and caesium 137 with a half-life of thirty-three years and emitting beta and gamma rays.

Strontium 90 is particularly dangerous because, due to its chemical similarity to calcium, an appreciable fraction is rapidly built into the bone, where it irradiates the bone marrow.[5] Our bones are not unchanging pieces of inert matter; they are living like the rest of the body and their constituent atoms are in constant flux. This has been established by studies with the radioactive isotope calcium 45. More new material is incorporated into the bones of growing children than into those of adults, so the strontium hazard is greater for them. Once strontium is incorporated in bone, it remains there for a long time. It tends to be concentrated in those parts of the bone that are growing most rapidly, and the irradiation in these areas may become sufficient to cause cancer of the bone.

The amount of strontium 90 present can be measured in strontium units, equal to one micromicrocurie of strontium per gram of calcium present. The maximum permissible level for strontium 90 in drinking water is 800 micromicrocuries per litre for small groups of people. During 1952–5, the radioactivity of the rainfall in Britain averaged 1·7 micromicrocuries per litre, which is well below the limit, even allowing for the tenfold reduction in permissible level usually made when whole populations are involved.

Continual measurements are made of the strontium 90 content of soils, plants, animals and food products. The results vary considerably with the district, being greater in areas of high rainfall and low calcium soil content. On the whole, the contamination is increasing with time, though it may be expected to level off and begin to fall if no further

[5] *ASJ*, 5, 405 (1956); *BAS*, 14, 62 (1958); R. E. Lapp, "Strontium Limits in Peace and War", *BAS*, 12, 287 (1956); J. M. Fowler (Ed.), *Fall-Out*, Basic Books, New York, 1960.

test explosions are made. So far, the amounts of strontium 90 are too small to constitute any appreciable hazard but the level certainly needs to be constantly checked.[6] It is particularly important to keep a careful check of the strontium 90 in milk, since this has a high calcium content, and is largely consumed by children, who are particularly susceptible to radiation damage. In the years 1954–6 the level rose from a very small value to between four and ten strontium units, depending on the locality.[7] Even if there are no further tests, it will continue to rise to about forty to fifty units around 1965, and thereafter will slowly fall.

Hazards from test explosions

In 1956 a committee was set up by the Atomic Scientists' Association under the chairmanship of Professor J. Rotblat to study the radiation hazards of test explosions. Its members included such distinguished medical specialists as Professor A. Haddow and Professor L. S. Penrose. They estimated that by 1970 the radiation dose to bone from the strontium 90 from the bomb tests will have risen to between one-tenth and half of that due to the natural background radiation.[8] This could cause bone cancer and leukemia in a small proportion of the population. If it is assumed that this is not a threshold phenomena, but that the effect is strictly proportional to the irradiation, they calculated that a hydrogen bomb of the type exploded at Bikini in March 1954 may eventually produce bone cancer in about 50,000 people. These casualties would be spread over the whole world and over several decades, and could not be distinguished among the vastly greater number

[6] *Strontium 90 in Human Diet in the United Kingdom*, 1958, H.M.S.O. The average diet for this year was $6\mu\mu C$ of Sr 90 per gram Ca, about a seventh of the level considered dangerous by the M.R.C.; J. Vaughan, "The Biological Behaviour of Strontium", *NS*, 5, 1080 (1959).

[7] A. Pirie (Ed.), *Fall-out*, MacGibbon and Kee, 1957, Ch. 6; J. M. Fowler, *loc. cit.*

[8] *BAS, 13*, 202 (1957).

of cases due to other causes. It is an exceedingly small fraction of the population of the world (less than one in 40,000) but is a substantial number of people. They emphasized that such estimates are highly uncertain and depend on a number of unproved assumptions. Nevertheless, they are the best that could be made, and it would seem prudent to accept them provisionally until more reliable estimates are available.

The radium content of soil is up to ten or more times the typical contamination by strontium 90, and the radiations it emits are more damaging. The additional hazard due to strontium 90 is thus much less than that existing already due to the natural radiation.

Two more radioactive isotopes among the fission products are iodine 131 with a half-life of eight days for beta-ray emission, and caesium 137 with a half-life of thirty-three years for 5 MeV gamma-ray emission. These are not so dangerous as strontium 90, but iodine 131 is concentrated in the thyroid gland of man and animals. Activities of several millimicrocuries of iodine 131 have been found in the thyroid glands of cattle. This is still very much smaller than the amounts known to lead to cancer of the thyroid, though little is known of the long-term effects. Caesium 137, like strontium 90, does not occur naturally, but due to the nuclear tests it is now to be found in our bodies. The gamma rays from it, though of lower energy, are already comparable in intensity to those we already receive from potassium 40.[9]

GENETIC EFFECTS

There has been hardly sufficient time to evaluate the genetic effects of nuclear explosions, as they only appear over many generations because most of the induced mutations are recessive. It is, therefore, necessary to rely on indirect evidence and the general principles of genetics to estimate them.

[9] A. Pirie (Ed.), *loc. cit.*, Chap. 7.

Japanese studies

Very careful studies have been made of the survivors of the Hiroshima and Nagasaki explosions to see if there was any evidence of increased malformation of their children. The conclusion of the British Medical Mission to Japan was that there was no evidence whatever for any type of genetic change, except perhaps for a slight change in the sex ratio.

From time to time, rumours have circulated about the many children being born in Japan with gross malformations due to the nuclear explosions. One of these, in 1955, was traced to an article in the Japanese Journal *Health and Midwifery* describing the abnormalities observed at 30,150 births attended by midwives in Nagasaki. They had apparently resolved to record every imperfection, however slight, and their list of abnormalities was a formidable one. It included, for example, 1,046 babies suffering from "degeneration of the bone, muscle, skin or nervous system". However, further investigation showed that approximately the same proportions of abnormalities were observed outside Nagasaki where there was no bombing. The babies in the category just mentioned included those having merely a wart. There was thus no basis whatever in these observations for ascribing any of the abnormalities to the nuclear explosions.[10]

This does not, however, provide any basis for complacency about the genetic effects of nuclear explosions. A more serious picture emerges when the genetic damage is established by more indirect methods. By the method outlined in Chapter III it has been estimated that an average exposure of about 2 roentgens per year over the whole population of the earth would double the natural mutation rate. Since the natural mutation rate is quite well known for many types of hereditary disease, and the average dose due to all the nuclear explosions to date can also be estimated, the damage done by these explosions can be found within rather large limits of error.

Whether we consider the incidence of bone cancer and

[10] Tano Jodai, "Report on Nagasaki Babies", *ASJ*, **4**, 289 (1955).

leukemia, or genetic damage, there is thus a startling contrast between the apparently insignificant increase in the background radiation due to the nuclear tests, and the large number of casualties that even this small increase may cause. This contrast makes it exceptionally difficult to consider the question in a balanced way, and accounts for the remarkable range of views on the subject and the apparently cogent arguments that can be used to support all of them.

Thus, if we want to make a case for the cessation of tests, it is easy to lay stress on the estimates of the tens of thousands of people who may be expected to suffer from leukemia as a result of the tests that have already taken place. The estimates may be a little uncertain, but it is better to be on the safe side. Others, equally correctly, point out that the tests have simply increased the natural radiation by a very small percentage. The chance of our suffering any harm from a one per cent increase in the natural radiation is exceedingly small. We have never worried about the existing hundred per cent, so why worry about the new one per cent? It is thus particularly easy for those whose minds have been made up on other grounds to find ample scientific evidence to make out an impressive case for their views.

This contrast between the small chance of danger to a selected individual and the certainty of many casualties over the whole population is not peculiar to the effects of nuclear radiations. It is found, for example, in the casualties due to road accidents and in many industrial processes. It is likewise found in many sports like cricket and football, and in amusements like letting off fireworks, where there is a small but finite chance of injury or even death. The question is whether or not to tolerate this danger for the undoubted benefits of the activity. This will be further discussed in Chapter VII, but it may be remarked that these problems of what may be called statistical morality are likely to be increasingly important in integrated modern societies, and deserve more attention from moral theologians than they have hitherto received.

CHAPTER VI

NUCLEAR WARFARE

It is not easy to translate our knowledge of destructive power into human terms and to envisage what happens when a nuclear bomb is exploded over an inhabited city. The sheer scale of the devastation, both of life and property, exceeds the most vivid imagination. Mere numbers of casualties and estimates of the area destroyed begin to lose their meaning even for those of us personally familiar with the not inconsiderable damage in the last war.

THE NUCLEAR BOMBING OF A CITY

Hiroshima and Nagasaki

Unhappily, we do not have to rely entirely on our imagination to assess the potentialities of nuclear weapons. Several personal accounts of experiences during and after the bombing of Hiroshima and Nagasaki have been published, and succeed in conveying something of the horror of these events.[1] The picture is not only of immense physical damage, of homes and shops and factories razed to the ground, not only of bodies shattered, burnt, irradiated and maimed for life,

[1] John Hersey, *Hiroshima*, Penguin Books No. 603, 1946; Takashi Nagai, *We of Nagasaki*, London, Gollancz, 1951; Fr Siemes, S.J., "Hiroshima—August 6th, 1945", *BAS*, *1*, No. 11, 2 (1946); M. Hachiya, *Hiroshima Diary*, University of North Carolina Press, 1955; R. Trumbull, *Nine who survived Hiroshima and Nagasaki*, New York, Dutton.

but also of intense psychological and spiritual trial.[2] Surrounded by the injured and the dying calling desperately for help, who, in a moment of unbearable stress, was not liable to think only of his own family and ignore the needs of a stranger, or put himself before even those closest to him? Though perhaps humanly speaking no more could be expected of him, yet the memory of appeals ignored, of cries unanswered, could remain to torment a survivor to the end of his days. The same can, of course, be said for large raids with high-explosive bombs, but the effects of nuclear bombing are unique due to the immense simultaneous destruction, and the fear of the unknown radiation effects.

Bomb damage

The extent of the damage depends on a large number of factors; the type of bomb, the height at which it is exploded, the weather, the configuration of the ground, the types of buildings, the degree of civil defence preparation and the amount of warning given.[3]

The type of bomb used determines the intensity of the heat flash and blast wave, and the degree of radioactive contamination. If it is exploded on the ground, the immediate vicinity will be more thoroughly devastated than if it had been exploded above the ground, but the area of the damage will not be so extensive, especially if undulations in the ground deflect the blast wave. On the other hand, if the bomb is exploded at a great height, a very large area will be less seriously damaged. There is thus an optimum height for

[2] I. L. Janis, "Psychological Problems of A-Bomb Defense", *BAS*, 6, 256 (1950); D. W. Chapman, "Some Psychological Problems in Civil Defense", *BAS*, 9, 280 (1953); P. Wylie, "Panic, Psychology and The Bomb", *BAS*, 10, 37 (1954); J. P. Spiegel, "Cry Wolf, Cry Havoc!" *BAS*, 10, 134 (1954); D. N. Michael, "Civilian Behavior under Atomic Bombardment", *BAS*, 11, 173 (1955); P. Wylie, "When Disaster Strikes", *BAS*, 12, 376 (1956), *BAS*, 13, 145 (1957).

[3] R. E. Lapp, "Atomic Bomb Explosions—Effects on an American City", *BAS*, 4, 49 (1948); "The Atomic Bomb and Our Cities" (*U.S. Strategic Bombing Survey*), *BAS*, 2, 3–4, 29 (1946).

doing the greatest damage with a bomb of given power; for a twenty-kiloton bomb it is about 2,000 feet, the height at which the Hiroshima bomb was exploded.

A ground explosion produces more radioactivity due to irradiation by the neutrons released in the chain reaction, and the extent of this induced radioactivity depends on the material irradiated. Explosion in the water of a harbour, for example, would be particularly dangerous, due to the formation of radioactive sodium and chlorine as well as the usual fission products, which would be spread over the town as a fine spray.

Damage to buildings

The weather mainly affects the heat flash; a little fog or mist can markedly reduce its intensity. The dryness of the ground and the closeness of the houses affects the spread of fires. Houses of light timber construction, like many of those in the stricken Japanese cities, are the most vulnerable. They are likely to be ignited by the heat flash and blown to splinters by the blast wave out to considerable distances from the explosion. Brick built structures are less liable to fire, but are readily crushed by blast. Light steel-framed industrial buildings are distorted bodily in the direction of the blast as if they had been pushed by a giant hand. Reinforced concrete buildings stand up remarkably well, especially if they are strengthened against earthquakes, as was the case for some of the Japanese buildings. They often remained structurally intact, while lighter surrounding buildings were razed to the ground.[4]

If the houses are very close together the many individual fires started by the fireball and heat flash and augmented by the blast may coalesce to form a fire storm. This burns so fiercely, fanned by winds of hurricane force coming in radially

[4] For detailed accounts of the structural damage, with illustrations, see *The Effects of the Atomic Bombs at Hiroshima and Nagasaki*, being the report of the British Mission to Japan, H.M.S.O., 1946.

from all directions, that there is no hope of checking it until all within its area is reduced to ashes.[5]

In the central area all buildings are shattered beyond repair by the blast wave alone, quite apart from the effects of subsequent fire. All the inhabitants are killed instantly, and the streets rendered impassable by rubble and fallen trees. This area presents no problem for Civil Defence; there is no one left to rescue and nothing left to save.

Farther out, there will be many survivors seriously injured and trapped in their wrecked houses. Since the rescue of one trapped person can well be an operation of some difficulty, requiring several trained men and their equipment, the majority of the trapped survivors will die long before help reaches them, unless the Civil Defence forces are numbered in thousands.

Casualties

Of those that are rescued, many will soon begin to show the symptoms of radiation sickness, and require skilled medical attention if they are to recover.[6] The hospitals and fire-fighting services of the stricken city are likely to be put out of action by the explosion itself, so help will have to come from neighbouring areas. These may well have been bombed themselves, or wish to retain their Civil Defence forces in case they are, and even if they decide to come would find it exceedingly difficult to penetrate to the more severely stricken areas due to the debris and streams of refugees already blocking the roads.[7]

In the outer areas there may well be hundreds of thousands of people requiring treatment for fractures, cuts and burns, and needing temporary repairs to their homes to prevent

[5] H. Bond, "Fire Storm Hazards", *BAS*, *9*, 277 (1953).

[6] A. W. Oughterson and S. Warren (Eds.), "Medical Effects of the Atomic Bomb in Japan", *BAS*, *13*, 35 (1957).

[7] E. C. Allen, "The Assessment of Atomic Casualties", *ASN*, *1*, 184 (1952).

further damage by the weather. There is little hope that any of this could be provided except from among themselves.

The long-term problems are just as serious. Without the most efficient evacuation to prepared, undamaged areas most of the injured will not receive the extended medical treatment they need. Most of the public utilities will be destroyed, gas-mains broken, electric power lines brought down, and water mains cracked. The distribution of food and water depends on the prompt influx of mobile relief columns on a large scale.[8]

Radioactivity

The hazard of radioactivity is likely seriously to disrupt the rescue operations. The whole area needs to be carefully monitored, so that rescue workers do not themselves receive dangerous doses. Open reservoirs and standing crops and vegetables will be contaminated and could only be consumed after thorough washing and examination for traces of radioactivity.[9] It may be unsafe to venture out of doors for more than a short period every day, until the radioactivity has decayed to a safe level.[10]

It has been estimated that about fifteen per cent of the casualties at Hiroshima and Nagasaki[11] were due to nuclear radiations. Since these radiations specially affect growing tissues, children unborn at the time of the explosion suffered severely. Miscarriages, embryonic and infant deaths, and mental retardation occurred with increased frequency.[12] Even

[8] V. Peterson, "Mass Evacuation", *BAS*, *10*, 294 (1954).

[9] I. Ogawa, "Fall-out and Rice Contamination in Japan", *BAS*, *14*, 35 (1958).

[10] W. G. Marley, "Radioactivity and Civil Defence", *ASN*, *1*, 193 (1952); Sir Claude Frankau, "The Casualty Service", *ASN*, *1*, 210 (1952).

[11] *The Effects of the Atomic Bombs at Hiroshima and Nagasaki*, H.M.S.O., 1946.

[12] J. N. Yamasaki *et al.*, "Outcome of pregnancy in women exposed to the atomic bomb in Nagasaki", *American Journal of Diseases of Children*, *87*, 448 (1954); J. V. Neel *et al.*, "The effect of exposure to the atomic bombs on pregnancy termination in Hiroshima and Nagasaki", *Science*, *118*, 537 (1953).

those who survived showed evidence, at the age of five years, of mental and physical retardation. Other effects of irradiation that have been noted among the survivors are cataract, temporary sterility and leukemia. In the years 1949–51 about fifty cases of leukemia were examined by the Atomic Bomb Casualty Commission; this is significantly greater than would be expected from a non-exposed population.[13]

CIVIL DEFENCE

While nothing short of impracticably deep shelters could do much for people in the central area, there are some Civil Defence measures that could do much to alleviate the injuries and damage in the outer areas. Unnecessary inflammable material could be removed from exposed positions, windows covered with netting or plastic to prevent flying glass, and light colours, which re-emit more of the incident radiation than dark ones, used wherever possible. Supplies of water and sand to fight small fires, first-aid material for the immediate treatment of injuries and plastic covering for temporary repairs could be kept available. A radiation monitor to measure the level of radioactivity and a few weeks' supply of food and water would aid survival during the critical period following the attack.

Not much can be done without prohibitive expense and inconvenience to strengthen ordinary brick-built houses against blast, but it is possible to increase the resistance of reinforced concrete buildings, and provide shelter area in the basements, for relatively little extra trouble.

Mobile rescue teams

The other side of Civil Defence consists of the mobile fire-fighting rescue and food columns which are stationed

[13] B. Black-Schaffer *et al.*, "Leukaemia in humans exposed to the Hiroshima and Nagasaki atomic bombs", *American Journal of Pathology, 28*, 548 (1952); J. H. Folley *et al.*, "Incidence of Leukaemia in survivors of the atomic bomb in Hiroshima and Nagasaki, Japan", *American Journal of Medicine, 13*, 311 (1952); N. Kusano (Ed.), *Atomic Bomb Injuries* (Tokyo, 1953).

ready to go to the aid of any bombed city. To have an appreciable effect these would need to be organized on a very large scale, and have thousands of vehicles and highly trained men.

The larger the bombs, the more inadequate these concepts of Civil Defence become. They are based essentially on the assumption that there will be relatively small areas of damage surrounded by unharmed territory. It is then mainly a matter of organizing rescue teams who will be prepared to move into the areas of damage immediately after the explosion and give what help they can to injured people and prevent further damage to property by fighting fires and by temporary repairs. This was certainly true in the last war, and is also true for attacks with a few atomic bombs, provided Civil Defence is organized on a nation-wide scale.[14]

It is unrealistic, however, to suppose that an attack if made would not be an all-out one aimed at simultaneously destroying most of the air bases and centres of population and industry with the most powerful hydrogen bombs available. Then the casualties could be numbered in tens of millions, and vast areas blanketed with a lethal or highly dangerous radioactive cloud.[15]

Fall-out

In the atomic bomb era, Civil Defence planners had to think in terms of the one- and three-mile circles of complete and partial damage. Now, with the multi-megaton hydrogen bombs, not only are these circles magnified up to ten times, but superposed on them are the vast ellipses, extending downwind for hundreds of miles and covering many thousands of square miles, of the radioactive fall-out.[16] In this context,

[14] H. Hart, "The Remedies versus The Menace", BAS, 10, 197 (1954).

[15] R. E. Lapp, "Nuclear War", and J. M. Fowler, "National Survival", Chs. 11 and 12 in Fall-Out (Ed. J. M. Fowler), Basic Books, New York, 1960.

[16] R. E. Lapp, "Civil Defense faces New Peril", BAS, 10, 349 (1954).

mobile Civil Defence rescue teams look like tackling a forest fire with a water pistol. No conceivable number of rescue teams could possibly be adequate to make a significant impact on the massive devastation.

It thus becomes clear that in a major attack it will be virtually every family for itself. No one can expect help from outside; any protective measures are the responsibility of each member of the population.[17]

Atomic shelters

Basically, there are two approaches to this, shelter or evacuation, the "get under" and the "get out".[18] There has been considerable difference of opinion on which of these is the most effective, and in any particular case it depends on the expected warning time, the concentration of the population and a number of secondary factors. Thus in Western Europe the most optimistic estimates of the warning time range from an hour or so for an airborne attack to a few minutes or less for a ballistic missile. Evacuation is then impossible and all that can be done is to get people under cover and underground as quickly as possible. Some countries, notably Sweden, have already constructed large underground shelters. Those in Stockholm, for example, are hewn out of solid rock, can hold upwards of 10,000 people, and are equipped with full feeding, air-filtering and sanitary facilities. A substantial part of the high capital cost has been recovered by using them in peacetime for storage and as car parks.[19] In other countries, like Western Germany, regulations are to be enforced concerning the provision of shelters in all new houses in large towns or cities.

[17] "Planning an Effective Civilian Defense", *BAS*, *10*, 291 (1954); R. J. Hopley, "Planning for Civil Defense", *BAS*, *5*, 111 (1949); H. Bond, "Military and Civil Confusion about Civil Defense", *BAS*, *5*, 295 (1949); Special Civil Defense issue, *BAS*, *6*, 225 (1950); "The Strategy of Civil Defense", *BAS*, *9*, 234 (1953).

[18] P. G. Steinbicker, "Shelter or Evacuation?" *BAS*, *13*, 166 (1957).

[19] M. M. Simpson, "A Long Hard Look at Civil Defense", *BAS*, *12*, 343 (1956).

The provision of such shelters for the majority of the population would be prohibitively expensive, but quite useful protection can be given by basements and small garden shelters. Shelters of this type would be of no value in the central region of complete destruction, but could substantially increase the chance of survival in peripheral regions.[20] They not only provide complete protection against the heat flash, and partial protection against the blast wave, but give considerable protection from the high levels of radioactivity that may be present during the first week after the explosions. Each foot of packed soil reduces the radiation to a tenth of its initial intensity, so quite moderate thicknesses would give adequate protection. The radioactivity from fall-out diminishes quite rapidly with time; seven hours after the explosion it is a tenth of what it was at one hour, after two days it is one-hundredth, after two weeks one-thousandth and after three months one-ten-thousandth.[21]

If the fission fall-out from a twelve-megaton bomb is spread over 6,000 square miles, the dose rate on the ground after one hour is about 5,000 roentgens per hour.[22] This is about ten times the lethal dose, but a small earth shelter would provide adequate protection, and after a few days the radiation level would have fallen enough to allow short times outside the shelter without undue hazard. If supplies of food had been stored in the shelter before the attack, the shelter would ensure the survival of a family through the period of

[20] R. E. Lapp, "Civil Defense Shelters", BAS, 14, 130 (1958).

[21] R. E. Lapp, "Radioactive Fall-out", BAS, 11, 45 (1955); "Fall-out and Candor", BAS, 11, 170, 206 (1955); A. H. Rosenfeld, E. J. Story, and S. D. Warshaw, "Fall-out: Measurements and Damage Estimates", BAS, 11, 213 (1955); W. F. Libby, "Radioactive Fall-out", BAS, 11, 256 (1955); R. E. Lapp, "Global Fall-out", BAS, 11, 339 (1955); "Fall-out from a Bombing Campaign", BAS, 14, 59 (1958); R. E. Lapp, "Fall-out", BAS, 15, 302 (1959); J. Schubert, "Fetal Irradiation and Fall-out", BAS, 15, 253 (1959).

[22] R. E. Lapp, "Local Fall-out Radioactivity", BAS, 15, 181 (1959); W. F. Libby, "Distribution and Effects of Fall-out", BAS, 14, 27 (1958).

intense radioactivity following the explosion. Such shelters were built in large numbers during the last war, but they were far from ideal when the enemy planes were overhead all night and every night for months on end. In these conditions the danger to health through dampness, overcrowding and loss of sleep was considerably greater than the dangeι from bombs. After a short spell in such shelters, many people decided they would be better off in their own beds. But in the conditions of a nuclear war, when the attack is likely to be short and sharp, such shelters could be of very real value.

Evacuation

In countries like the United States, which can expect to have about four to six hours' warning of an airborne attack from its ring of Arctic radar stations, evacuation becomes a practicable alternative to shelters, though it does not entirely supplant them. With sufficient wide roads and preliminary organization, a fair-sized city can be substantially evacuated in a couple of hours.[23] There will be some additional casualties because many people will be caught in the open by the explosion, but on balance evacuation will save lives. One of the disadvantages of such schemes is that if an enemy discovers that people will stream out of all the cities as soon as a plane appears on radar screens thousands of miles away it will simply send a plane along every day. The disorganization caused by constant evacuations would in itself amount to severe damage.

Extensive studies of the Civil Defence problems have been made in the United States. A Congressional Committee headed by Congressman C. Holifield made an exhaustive survey and presented its report in 1956.[24] They found that pitifully little was being done, the agencies responsible not having grasped the realities of the situation, or succeeded in

[23] V. Peterson, "Mass Evacuation", *BAS, 10*, 294 (1954).
[24] M. M. Simpson, *loc. cit.*; C. Holifield, "Civil Defence", Ch. 9 in *Fall-Out* (Ed. J. M. Fowler), Basic Books, New York, 1960.

obtaining essential facts from the A.E.C., which displayed an alarming optimism about the effects of nuclear explosions. It looked as if the task was so complicated and costly that there was no practicable solution, but instead of saying so a phantom programme had been started to give people the impression that something useful was being done.

The Committee found that constructive Civil Defence measures could be taken. One of the witnesses, Dr M. Tuve of the National Academy of Sciences, thought that "a civilian defence effort costing several billion dollars and spread out over a few years may mean a difference of 60 million casualties or more in the event of an all-out war". The final Report put the cost at $2B to $3B per year for six years to accomplish the primary tasks of Civil Defence. They concluded that an effective Civil Defence is an integral part of a nation's ability to deter war and to survive one if it comes.[25]

An unprepared nation would feel itself so vulnerable that it would hesitate to retaliate in the event of an attack and this in itself would make it more liable to be attacked.

Dispersal of industries

A long-term Civil Defence project is the gradual dispersal of vital industries. At present they tend in most countries to be concentrated in a few areas. This has great economic advantages, but could be a source of weakness in a nuclear war. Efforts have been made, notably in the United States, to encourage new industries to seek to establish themselves away from the main industrial areas.[26] This policy soon

[25] A. W. Bellamy and S. L. Warren, "National Survival in the Atomic Age", *BAS, 15*, 390 (1959); R. E. Lapp, "What is the Price of Nuclear War?" *BAS, 15*, 340 (1959).

[26] J. Marshak, E. Teller, and L. R. Klein, "Dispersal of Cities and Industries", *BAS, 1*, No. 9, 13 (1946); T. B. Augur, "The Dispersal of Cities as a Defense Measure", *BAS, 4*, 131, 312 (1948); T. B. Augur, "Dispersal is Good Business", *BAS, 6*, 244 (1950); D. and A. Monson, "A Program for Urban Dispersal", *BAS, 7*, 244 (1951); R. E. Merriam, "Cities are Here to Stay", *BAS, 7*, 251 (1951); R. E. Lapp, "Industrial

becomes involved in politics, and in most cases heavy Government subsidies would be needed to offset the disadvantages, so that very little has been achieved in this direction.

ACTIVE DEFENCE

The most valuable form of defence is to prevent the bombs being dropped at all by camouflage or decoy or by shooting the attacking bombers down before they reach their target. This became increasingly practicable during the last war due to the development of night fighters equipped with radar. If only about ten to twenty per cent of the attacking force was destroyed, it soon became impossible for the enemy to sustain the attack over a long period of time. Likewise, a large fraction of the V1 pilotless aircraft were destroyed by a combination of balloons, anti-aircraft fire and fighter planes. Providing the defending force had not lost control of the air, it could exact a heavy toll from enemy bombing forces.

The situation is quite different now. The bombers can fly at supersonic speeds high in the stratosphere and even if only one or two of them get through they can inflict crippling damage with nuclear bombs. It is not sufficient to shoot down twenty per cent of the attacking force; even ninety-five per cent is not enough. In spite of intensive development of surface-to-air and air-to-air guided missiles they are still not efficient enough to guarantee one hundred per cent kills in all circumstances.[27]

Dispersion in the United States", *BAS*, 7, 256 (1951); "Industrial Dispersion as a National Policy", *BAS*, 7, 265 (1951); R. Bolling, "Politics in Dispersal", *BAS*, 7, 278 (1951); A. H. Hawley, "Urban Dispersal and Defense", *BAS*, 7, 307 (1951); A. Mayer, "The Need for Synchronized Dispersal", *BAS*, 8, 49 (1952); "Dispersal of American Industry", *BAS*, 10, 196 (1954); D. Monson, "Is Dispersal Obsolete?" *BAS*, 10, 378 (1954); B. H. Zimm, "Dispersion along the Mohawk", *BAS*, 11, 178 (1955).

[27] J. R. Killian and A. G. Hill, "For a Continental Defense", *BAS*, 10, 13 (1954).

Ballistic missiles

The possibilities of effective defence are even less against ballistic missiles. Even in the last war, it was impossible to stop the V2 rockets once they were on their way. All that could be done was to attack the laboratories where they were designed, the factories where they were made, and the sites from which they were launched. This is still true now, except for some rather fanciful ideas about interception missiles equipped with nuclear warheads and sent up to destroy the oncoming missile before it re-enters the earth's atmosphere. This is an almost impossible problem technically, as the missiles are coming almost vertically downwards at several thousand m.p.h. It is equally difficult to destroy the launching sites, as they may be small well-hidden underground concrete pads up to 5,000 miles away, or submarines that could launch their missiles within a few hundred miles of most European and American cities. There is now a considerable range of missiles from the solid-fuel short-range army weapons to the giant liquid-fuelled 5,000-miles-range ICBM's.[28]

The result of these technological developments is that at present there is no hope of effective defence against a major power, and no new advances can be foreseen that could alter this situation. For the same reasons, there is no chance of destroying an enemy's retaliatory potential in a single unexpected blow.

THE STRATEGY OF NUCLEAR WARFARE

During the last fifteen years, extensive studies have been made of the strategy of nuclear warfare, with the object of coming to grips with the problems that could confront statesmen

[28] R. Rollefson, "Why so many Missiles?" *BAS, 13*, 295 (1957); M. M. Simpson, *The Race for Missiles*; A. Shternfeld, *Soviet Space Science*, Basic Books, New York, 1959; H. M. Jackson, "The Increasing Threat of Ballistic Missiles", *BAS, 12*, 90 (1956); T. Margerison, "Missiles to Stop Missiles?" *NS, 5*, 733 (1959).

and service chiefs in time of war.[29] Army exercises have been conducted assuming both sides to possess nuclear weapons. In the early days these were frequently used so liberally that umpires had to declare all life extinct over wide areas.

Limitation of nuclear war

Considerable attention has been given to the problem of limiting nuclear warfare. Would it be possible to use small tactical nuclear weapons to repel an invading army without precipitating an all-out nuclear strategic assault on the centres of population? In Britain, continuing studies of these and related problems have been made under the auspices of the Institute of Strategic Studies, an organization that began in 1957 as a result of a Conference devoted to the practicability of limiting nuclear war.[30] The consensus of opinion is that there can be no sure way of confining nuclear war to the battlefield.

It is therefore urged that it is unwise to rely too heavily on nuclear weapons for defence; it might prove difficult to use them without causing strategic reprisals. Attacks with non-nuclear forces are more safely repulsed by conventional weapons. It is possible that the West has been unwise to rely on tactical nuclear weapons for defence against all forms of attack, and to so reduce conventional weapons that the nuclear weapons would have to be used, and used first, to repel an aggressor.

[29] "Science and Military Strategy", *BAS, 12,* May/June 1956; P. M. S. Blackett, *Military and Political Consequences of Atomic Energy,* Turnstile Press, 1948.
[30] "On Limiting Atomic War", *BAS, 13,* 216 (1957).

CHAPTER VII

THE MORALITY OF NUCLEAR WARFARE

Ever since the first atomic bombs were dropped, there has been intense discussion of the morality of their use. Their vast destructive power, their radioactive effects and their indiscriminate action have all been cited to show the uniqueness of the moral problems they raise. Discussion of moral problems *per se* is beyond the scope of this book, but since the application of moral principles to a particular situation depends on the facts of the case, it is relevant to consider how traditional Christian moral principles may be applied to the problems posed by the application of nuclear energy, both in peace and in war.

BASIC MORAL PRINCIPLES

The morality of an act depends partly on the intrinsic nature of the act and partly upon its foreseeable consequences. No act that is intrinsically evil is permissible, however good its consequences may be. Thus no argument can justify the direct killing of the innocent. There is no need even to inquire into the consequences; whatever they are the act remains immoral.

The situation is more complex for intrinsically good or neutral acts. Here the probable consequences have to be weighed and if the intended good consequences outweigh the unwanted evil ones the act is permissible; if they do not it is not. This is sometimes known as the principle of the double effect, but it is essentially a technique of moral analysis.[1]

Applications

These principles are not easy to apply in practice. How, for example, is the act to be distinguished from its consequences? Must there be a temporal or a spatial interval, or both? How can the good and evil consequences of an act be estimated and compared? The most we can expect from a moral analysis of our actions is that some may be shown to be clearly inadmissible, for they can only be justified by arguments that lead to evident wrong in other contexts, some again may be justified because their converse is inadmissible. In between these limiting cases there will be a region where no clear-cut answer can be given. Each individual can only use his judgement and experience to decide what to do, and be answerable to God for his decision.

PEACEFUL USES OF ATOMIC ENERGY

It is convenient to begin by considering some of the moral problems raised by the peaceful applications of atomic energy. These have not received the attention devoted to the morality of nuclear warfare, but are none the less important and likely to face increasing numbers of people. They are perhaps not so complex, and thus provide the easiest starting point for coming to grips with moral problems of the atomic age.

Important problems have arisen due to the effects of nuclear radiations on the human body. Peaceful uses of atomic energy can, and sometimes will, inevitably cause some irradiation of people, and this irradiation is almost always harmful. Whether this harm can be justified must be considered in each particular case.

[1] For a fuller discussion see D. J. B. Hawkins, *Man and Morals,* Sheed and Ward, London and New York, 1960, especially Ch. VI.

Natural irradiation

Irradiation of the human body is no new thing; indeed there has never been a time when man has not been exposed to nuclear radiation, from the radioactive substances in his own body, in the soil and from cosmic radiation. The intensity of this natural radiation varies greatly from place to place. In general igneous rocks like granite and anything containing uranium or radium can have a high radioactive content, while sedimentary rocks have very little. The cosmic radiation is progressively absorbed as it comes down through the earth's atmosphere so it is more intense at high altitudes than at sea level. Although a substantial fraction of the deleterious mutations suffered by man are due to this natural radiation, its effect on the population as a whole is exceedingly small. It forms a convenient indication of the level of radiation that can be tolerated indefinitely by the average human body without significant somatic damage.

It cannot, therefore, be held that the hazard of nuclear radiation is such that we are morally obliged to keep it to a minimum, irrespective of all other considerations. This would imply the absurdity of living at sea level, or even underground, in regions of low radioactive soil content, and never venturing beyond them.

Medical uses of nuclear radiation

Serious problems arise in the medical use of nuclear radiations. Irradiation of a malignant tumour may be necessary to save or prolong life, and yet at the same time there is danger of genetic damage. If the patient is over the usual reproductive age there is no problem, but it is otherwise for a young person. A similar problem arises in X-ray pelvimetry when, if a difficult birth is expected, accurate measurements may be made beforehand by X-rays, thus facilitating the birth, yet incurring a danger of genetic damage and increased susceptibility to leukemia. Again, during mass X-radiography of the chest to detect tuberculosis there is a small but definite gonad dose that could cause genetic damage.

There are many cases like these when the application of nuclear radiations brings urgently desired benefits yet also causes damage. They fall into the class of problems covered by the principle of the double effect, and so the radiations may be used if the anticipated good outweighs the unwanted damage. Providing all the facts are determined as far as possible, the decision lies with the medical specialist.

Abuses

It is quite another matter when nuclear radiations are used for relatively trivial purposes, such as the use of X-rays for shoe-fitting. It has been found that some shoe-fitting machines bathe not only the feet but also a substantial part of the body with a dangerous amount of radiation. Another example is the use of X-rays for the removal of unwanted hair. A case is on record of a lady whose arms were irradiated for this purpose, and the radiation damage was so extensive that they subsequently had to be amputated.[2] Cases such as this certainly took place in the past through ignorance, but now that more is known the continuing use of radiation for trivial purposes is criminal.

Safety precautions

Whenever the radiations are used for a justifiable medical purpose, the apparatus must be shielded so that no unnecessary radiations escape, and the dose must be carefully measured and limited strictly to the amount required. Even now, when the dangers of indiscriminate irradiation are well understood, there are frequent cases of unnecessary irradiation. Strict supervision of the manufacture and use of machines producing radiations for medical use is a continu-

[2] J. Schubert and R. E. Lapp, *Radiation*, Heinemann, 1957, p. 16. See also Ch. V for details of many similar incidents.

ing necessity. Similar supervision is required wherever radiation is used in industry or in research.

Nuclear power stations

Some moral problems are also associated with the siting of nuclear power stations. Although the reactors they contain are designed so carefully that there is no danger of an accidental nuclear explosion, there is an exceedingly small chance of an excessive leak of radioactivity due to overheating, faulty fuel elements and failure of the filtering system.[3] It is therefore desirable to build the power stations away from densely populated areas, where the consequences of such an unlikely accident can be easily dealt with, and yet not so far that it would be too costly to transport the electricity generated to where it is required. Another requirement is the proximity of plentiful water supplies for cooling the reactors and an outlet for radioactive waste so that it can be disposed of without hazard. In a relatively small country like Great Britain, this severely limits the choice of suitable sites, and whichever one is chosen is likely to arouse protests that private property is threatened, unspoilt countryside desecrated, bird sanctuaries destroyed and so on. This sort of problem arises frequently in modern societies, for example when railways are being built, and the work may be justified for the common good provided that due notice is given, objections heard and compensation made.

The development of nuclear power stations fortunately does not always desecrate the beauties of nature. As they are not dependent on the proximity of coal supplies, they can be sited within reach of centres of population far removed from coal fields. This is the case for the Dungeness and Berkeley (Gloucestershire) power stations, which have removed the need for more overhead power lines coming down from the Midlands. Nuclear power, as it becomes cheaper, will also render hideous gas-works and slag heaps obsolete. These

[3] An example of this is the Windscale incident.

consequences of the change to nuclear power stations cannot fail to please all interested in preserving the amenities of the countryside.

NUCLEAR WARFARE

Turning now to the morality of nuclear warfare, a brief summary must first be given of the traditional Christian teaching on the morality of war in general.[4] It has always been recognized that war is an immense evil, bringing in its train destruction of life, property and the right order of society. There is no greater international crime than that of starting a war of aggression solely to subjugate a neighbouring nation, occupy its territory, seize its treasures and enslave its peoples.

The just war

But war is not an absolute evil, to be avoided at all costs. A nation that is unjustly attacked has, in certain circumstances, the right and even the duty to fight back in defence of its life. Very grave reasons are required to justify a nation going to war. The threat must be of the utmost gravity that strikes at its very existence, and every effort must be made to resolve the dispute by peaceful negotiation, with the arbitration of a third party if necessary. The defensive action taken must be only what is necessary to repel the aggressor and restore peace, and remains itself bound by the moral law.

Right of self-defence

A comparison is sometimes made between the rights of self-defence of an individual and of a nation. An individual

[4] For more detailed accounts, see J. Eppstein (Ed.), *Code of International Ethics,* Sands, 1952; H. Davis, S.J., *Moral Theology,* Vol. II, Sheed and Ward; J. Eppstein, *The Catholic Tradition of the Law of Nations.* For the legal aspects of nuclear warfare, see Nagendra Singh, *Nuclear Weapons and International Law,* Stevens, 1959; G. Schwarzenberger, *The Legality of Nuclear Weapons,* 1958.

is justified in defending himself, but if the attack is directed against himself personally, it may be, as a counsel of perfection, better not to resist. This does not apply to a whole nation, since in this case there is also the Christian duty of going to the aid of those who are unable to defend themselves. A Government cannot be as free with the rights of the community it was elected to defend as an individual may be with some of his personal rights. It is an act of perfection to accept and forgive injuries done to ourselves, but it is a vice to tolerate injuries done to our neighbour, if we are able to defend him.

In his 1956 Christmas address, Pius XII said:

> It is clear that in present circumstances a situation could come about in which, every effort to avoid it having been made in vain, war, for effective self-defence and with the hope of a favourable outcome against unjust attack, could not be considered unlawful. If, therefore, a body representative of the people and a government decides, in a moment of extreme danger, by legitimate instruments of internal and external policy, on defensive precautions, and carry out the plans they consider necessary, they do not act immorally. Therefore, a Catholic citizen cannot invoke his own conscience in order to refuse to serve and fulfil those duties the law imposes.[5]

Conduct of hostilities

The actual conduct of a war poses agonizing moral problems. The Christian tradition has always insisted on the distinction between combatants and non-combatants. The latter include children, the aged and infirm and those in occupations not directly connected with the hostilities. These people may not be directly attacked in any circumstances for this would be an intrinsically evil act. This distinction was fairly clear-cut in the past, but in modern times has become increasingly blurred as more and more of the population become involved in the war effort. Nevertheless, it is not

[5] *Acta Apostolicae Sedis*, XLIX, 19 (1957).

blurred out of existence, and even in modern total war a substantial fraction of the population must still be classed as
non-combatants.

With war confined to the battlefield, it was not too difficult
to confine hostilities to combatants, though the indirect effects
of war, famine, disease and civil disorder inevitably tended to
engulf whole populations. Now, however, war in the air ranges
over the whole territory of the nations at war, and often over
that of neutrals as well. The munitions factories, power
stations, bridges and railways of the enemy then become
legitimate objects of attack. But they are often intermingled
with people's homes and other buildings devoted to peaceful
purposes, and the question arises of how to destroy the one
without harming the other. Here again the principle of the
double effect may be applied and the factory or other target
attacked, even if it is foreseen that this will probably result
in unwanted injury of non-combatants and destruction of
their homes. The bombing is justified by the good effect of
halting the production of offensive weapons, and the evil
effect on non-combatants reluctantly tolerated. Modern bombing thus imposes severe obligations on those responsible for
it. Every effort must be made to ensure that the minimum
damage is done to non-combatants. This is an extraordinarily
difficult problem, as the enemy is undoubtedly doing all he
can to hinder the attack by fighter planes, anti-aircraft fire,
searchlights, blackout and camouflage, and the commander
of the attack has to conserve his forces as far as possible. It
is so much easier, especially with nuclear weapons, to obliter-
ate the whole city, factories and houses, combatants and non-
combatants, all together with one bomb. This, however, would
be immoral, except perhaps in the case of a town exclusively
devoted to arms production.

The ease with which legitimate targets may be identified
and attacked is frequently overestimated in discussions of the
morality of bombing, so that they become completely unrealistic. It was found at the beginning of the last war that

pilots had the greatest difficulty in finding out where they were. Sometimes they did not know what country they were over, let alone what town. The accuracy of position finding improved as the war progressed, however, especially with the development of radar and the Pathfinder technique. It is now much more practicable, but still not easy, to pin-point particular targets.

Nuclear weapons

The morality of the use of nuclear weapons may be considered in just the same way as that of other weapons, though it is complicated by the immensely greater range of destructive power available, and by the radioactive effects. There is no ground for drawing a sharp distinction between the two; if it is legitimate to destroy an army or munitions factory with a hundred high-explosive bombs, then it is legitimate to do it with one nuclear bomb.[6] The added factor of radioactivity must be weighed along with the other unwanted effects of the action. As mentioned above, there is no ground for maintaining that the evil effects of radiation are so great that no increase of radiation intensity can ever be tolerated. It is, of course, necessary whenever possible to use the "cleanest" type of bomb that produces the smallest radioactive contamination for the desired explosive effect.

[6] A discussion of the morality of the atomic bombing of Hiroshima and Nagasaki is beyond the scope of this book. The following may be consulted for historical accounts of the decision and discussions of its morality: A. H. Compton, *Atomic Quest*, Oxford, 1956; G. E. M. Anscombe, *Mr. Truman's Degree*; "Before Hiroshima", *BAS, 1* 10 (1946); H. L. Stimson, "The Decision to use the Bomb", *BAS, 3,* 2, p. 37 (1947); A. M. Brues, "With the Atomic Casualty Commission in Japan", *BAS, 3,* 143 (1947); A. H. Compton and F. Daniels, "A Poll of Scientists at Chicago, July 1945", *BAS, 4,* 44 (1948); A. K. Smith, "Behind the Decision to use the Atomic Bomb: Chicago, 1944–45", *BAS, 14,* 288 (1958); M. Amrine, *The Great Decision*, Putnams, New York, 1959; *BAS, 15,* 221 (1959); J. F. C. Fuller, *The Decisive Battles of the Western World, 3,* 624 (1956); H. L. Stimson, "The Decision to Use the Atomic Bomb", *Harper's Magazine* (1947).

Atomic and hydrogen bombs

From the moral point of view, it cannot be maintained that atomic bombs are sometimes justifiable but that hydrogen bombs are not. Both types can now be made over a large and overlapping range of destructive powers; the atomic bomb ranging from 500 tons to 500,000 tons* and the hydrogen bomb from 100,000 tons to 30 megatons,* all these figures being approximate. All the power of an atomic bomb comes from the fission process, with its associated radioactive hazard. Only a small proportion of the power of a hydrogen bomb comes from fission. Thus in the region where their powers overlap, a hydrogen bomb would cause less radioactivity than an atomic bomb of the same power. It would thus, if a suitable target presented itself, be morally desirable to use the hydrogen bomb and not the atomic bomb. So when moral questions are being considered the important factors are the power of the bomb and the proportion of that power that is derived from fission, which gives a measure of the radioactive hazard. Once this is known, the actual mechanism of the bomb is irrelevant.

It is not practicable to distinguish between the two types of bombs by their destructive power, saying that hydrogen bombs are so powerful that there could never be any legitimate target for them. As mentioned above, they are now made over a wide range of explosive powers, and it is not difficult to imagine suitable targets for the less powerful ones. A fleet at sea or a widely dispersed military base or munitions dump in an uninhabited region are obvious examples. Even the larger ones could perhaps be justifiably used to produce a powerful underwater explosion to destroy lurking enemy submarines over a wide area.

The indiscriminate nature of the widespread effects of nuclear explosions restricts the targets on which they may be justifiably used. The wide range of explosive powers now available makes it possible to select the power sufficient to

* TNT equivalent.

destroy the target without causing superfluous damage. There is no justification for the indiscriminate use of the largest bomb, whatever the size of the target.

Pius XII on nuclear warfare

The morality of nuclear warfare was frequently alluded to in the addresses of Pius XII, in which he applied the traditional teaching of the Church to current problems.[7] He reiterated that because of the sufferings caused by modern war it was not justified unless it were indispensable for defence against a clear and extremely grave injustice. Every effort must be made to avoid or limit such a war and

> if, despite these efforts, the setting in motion of an ABC (atomic, bacteriological and chemical) war meant that it would bring in its wake such widely spread evil effects as were completely beyond human control, then its use would have to be rejected as immoral, for it would then be a case not just of defence against injustice, but of annihilation of all human life within the radius of the destructive action, which was not permissible on any account.[8]

This Address has rightly received considerable attention, and there has been some discussion of the meaning of the expression "beyond human control". It would seem that a weapon could be described as "controllable" if the effects of

[7] A useful collection and summary of these addresses is given by M. M. Feeny, *Just War?* (Sword of the Spirit pamphlet, 1958). In these addresses the Pope does not enunciate any new doctrine; he simply restates and develops what has always been the teaching of the Church. They are not of course infallible but derive special authority from the eminence of their author. For an account of the status of papal addresses, and the extent and limit of their authority, see C. Journet, *The Church of the Word Incarnate*, Sheed and Ward, 1959. There are numerous other discussions of the morality of nuclear warfare, among which may be noted: I. Hislop and L. Bright, *Black-friars, 37*, 100 (1956); "Symposium on the Morality of Nuclear Warfare", *ASJ, 4*, 3 (1954); "The Christian Conscience and Weapons of Mass Destruction", *BAS, 7*, 115 (1951); *The Church and the Atom*, Publications Board of the Church Assembly, Westminster, 1948.

[8] Address to the Eighth Congress of the World Medical Association on 30th September, 1954. *Acta Apostolicae Sedis* XLVI-II-xxi, pp. 587 ff. *Documentation Catholique*, No. 1183.

its action are limited and known to the user. A weapon would be uncontrolled if its effects spread indiscriminately outward like a divergent chain reaction, causing destruction or disease to an extent quite unknown to the user of the weapon. In spite of the destructive power of nuclear weapons, and the extensive nature of the physical and biological damage they cause, it would seem that they could be considered controllable because, although great, the extent of the damage can be estimated within certain limits, which is all that can be required for any weapon. Even the somatic and genetic effects, though they may not appear until long after the actual explosion, can be approximately estimated. There is no question of damage spreading out uncontrollably to engulf more and more people.

If it is legitimate for nuclear weapons to be used in self-defence, then it is also legitimate to manufacture them in times of peace if there is a possibility of war breaking out. This is certainly the case at present, when in the words of Pius XII:

> nations must reckon with unprincipled criminals who, in order to realize their ambitious plans, were not afraid to unleash total war. That was the reason why all countries, if they wished to preserve their very existence and their most precious possessions, and unless they were prepared to accord free action to international criminals, had no alternative but to prepare for the day when they must defend themselves. This right to be ready for self-defence could not be denied in these days to any state.[9]

Later, he emphasized the right of self-defence still further, observing:

> Today war is no longer confined to engaged battle between armed men but has stretched to a point where a conflict is

[9] Address to the Fourteenth International Congress of Penal Law on October 3rd, 1953, *Acta Apostolicae Sedis* XLV-II-xx, pp. 730 ff. *Documentation Catholique*, No. 1159; Catholic Documents, Pontifical Court Club, Salesian Press, No. XIV.

between peoples, wherein are mobilized all physical and moral energies, all economic and industrial resources. It is no longer a field of battle, the whole state is an arena of war and the weapons prepared are of unimaginable power. The problem of national defence therefore takes on a new and increasing importance, and so does the problem of its solution. This is the reason why no nation that wished to provide, as was its undoubted right and duty, for the security of its frontiers, can do without an army proportioned to its needs, which lacks nothing that is indispensable for effective action, ready and alert in case it should be unjustly threatened and attacked.[10]

Tests of nuclear weapons

Over the last decade the intensive development of military strategy geared to a whole range of tactical nuclear weapons has made them indispensable for effective defence.[11] If such weapons are to be made and held in readiness, the new types must be periodically tested. As the development of nuclear weapons proceeds, it becomes possible to increase the explosive power obtainable from a given amount of fissile material, to reduce the radioactive hazard, and to improve their reliability and ease of delivery. It is not at all a matter of making bombs more and more powerful; rather the aim is to increase their compactness and efficiency so that they may be more precisely suited to their targets. As this development proceeds, it is necessary to carry out periodic tests to check the validity of new methods of detonation, and the accuracy of the calculations of the power released. The justification of a particular test depends on the importance of the new data that the test is designed to supply, balanced against the damage that the test will probably cause, even if it takes place in a remote region. Most of this information is inevitably classified as secret, which makes it usually impossible to decide whether a particular test is justified or not.

---

[10] Address published in *Osservatore Romano*, May 22nd, 1958. *Documentation Catholique*, No. 1279.
[11] E. Teller, "The Nature of Nuclear Warfare", *BAS, 13,* 162 (1957).

The dangers of nuclear tests are such that very grave reasons are needed to justify them. The Bikini test showed that direct radioactive hazards are considerable even at distances of a hundred miles or more from the explosion. These consequences of test explosions show the care that needs to be taken before they are made. More recent tests have been almost free from radioactive contamination, and it is likely that the development of underground test procedures will eventually remove this hazard entirely.

The hazards of nuclear tests led to a widespread campaign for their cessation.[12] This was particularly strong in Japan, because the Japanese had suffered not only from the two atomic bombs during the war, but also from the Pacific and Siberian tests. In April 1957, the Japanese sent a special envoy to Pius XII to ask his intervention to stop the nuclear tests. In reply the Pope deplored the useless waste of scientific activity in the arms race, and urged men of all nations to join together to harness atomic energy to the service of mankind.[13] He did not, however, directly condemn the nuclear tests on this or on any other occasion. There is no ground for the widespread belief that he did so.

Pacifism

There is a considerable body of opinion that is prepared to admit that the use of small atomic weapons may, in some rather abstract circumstances, be morally justified, but that in the present concrete situation they will almost certainly be used immorally. It is one of the lessons of history that nations at war, especially if they are facing defeat, will use every weapon they have, irrespective of moral considerations.[14]

[12] "The Bomb Test Controversy", *BAS*, *12*, 322 (1956).
[13] Note to Professor Matsatoki Matsushita, April 14th, 1957; *Osservatore Romano*, April 24th, 1957; *Documentation Catholique*, No. 1251; *The Tablet*, May 4th, 1958.
[14] The belligerents in the 1939–45 war refrained from using poison gas not because of any moral scruples, but partly for fear of retaliation in kind and partly because it is, in any case, a rather ineffective weapon. See also L. Hartley, "False Parallel", *BAS*, *6*, 172 (1950).

During the last war, powers that began by dropping leaflets ended by indiscriminate mass destruction raids aimed at destroying enemy life, morale and property. The psychological effect of receiving a nuclear weapon, even a small tactical one, is likely to be so great that the stricken people will demand immediate retaliation, with the most powerful bombs available, on the enemy's centres of population. Furthermore, some of the policy statements of Western politicians, and still more of military leaders, have been couched in language asserting that any aggression would be met by instant and massive retaliation. So seriously is this threat meant that loaded bombers are continually in the air, fully prepared to fly to preassigned targets and drop their deadly burdens. In such a situation, it is argued, when nuclear war will certainly lead to immoral actions on an unprecedented scale, the Christian has no option but to contract out of the whole terrifying affair.

There are, however, a number of considerations that tend to weaken these arguments. The military leaders have had sufficient time now to think through the conditions prevailing in a nuclear war to be able to decide beforehand on what they will do in certain foreseeable sets of circumstances. They are not likely to be deflected from this at the last minute by mob hysteria. They are by now only too well aware of the serious consequences of any decision they make.

One of the unpleasant features of modern diplomacy is the growing separation between what is known as the "declaratory policy" and the actual policy. In other words, there is frequently a clear distinction between what statesmen say they intend to do, and what they will actually do. In the present case, there is a noticeable tendency for the declaratory policy to be much more uncompromising and aggressive than the real one. Some subtlety is needed to penetrate to the real meaning behind the words. No nation is obliged to give precise details in advance of what it intends to do if it is attacked; what it can do is to state uncompromisingly that it intends to defend itself with all the means at its disposal. Provided no definitely immoral action is specifically promised, we are entitled to presume that the defence will be conducted according to the moral law. There is far more likelihood that this will in fact be done if Christians play their full part in preparing for the justified defence of their country than if they contract out of it altogether.

CHAPTER VIII

THE INTERNATIONAL CONTROL OF ATOMIC ENERGY

The present international situation, with two power blocs each capable of destroying the other at short notice, cannot fail to cause universal anxiety, and to encourage every attempt at its resolution. The gulf between the beliefs and ways of life of the opposing peoples is so deep that no easy solution can be expected; at best it will be the task of many decades.

EAST–WEST TENSION

The separation between the Eastern and Western blocs is not a simple one; many Christian peoples are ruled by Communist régimes, and a large proportion of Westerners live materialistic lives untouched by the Christianity that was originally one of the main bases of our civilization. Apart from the opposing blocs, there are many neutral nations more or less sympathetic to one or other of them. There are also the uncommitted nations of Africa and Asia, avid for material development, who are more likely to be impressed by technological achievements than by concepts of democracy and freedom that they have never experienced.

While the nations are agreed in wanting to exploit the

material advances made possible by modern science, there is fundamental disagreement on the way this is to be done, a disagreement that goes much deeper than the purely economic and technical level. Both Christianity and Communism are revolutionary, dynamic beliefs that aim to remould the whole of human society, and cannot accept any limits to their world-wide expansion.

This conflict inevitably puts severe strains on international relations. With the rapidity of modern communications small disputes can readily flare up into open conflict. Larger nations can swiftly rally to the support of smaller ones, soon precipitating a widespread struggle. Outside Europe, some of the smaller nations have not yet developed a stable and respected constitutional government, backed by a mature and intelligent electorate. Democratic government, however benevolently planted by departing colonial powers, finds it difficult to survive in the atmosphere of new-found exultant nationalism. Moderate governments are forced to adopt sterner measures if they are to survive, and are frequently supplanted by powerful individuals who willingly assume dictatorial powers in the name of the people. To maintain their power, increasingly severe restrictions are imposed on internal freedom, and a suspicious and intransigent attitude is adopted towards other nations.

The risk of nuclear war

While the main power blocs seem to be sufficiently mature and aware of the consequences not to risk any action that might lead to war, the same cannot be said of many of the smaller nations. Insecure dictators might easily feel themselves obliged by circumstances they have themselves created to undertake actions that could lead to a small conflict. Larger nations could soon become involved due to existing treaties and agreements. As nuclear weapons become no longer the monopoly of two or three powers they will increasingly come into the hands of irresponsible régimes who would not hesitate to use them to solve an immediate crisis, irrespective of the ultimate consequences. A war without nuclear weapons would be severe enough, but with them could be an unimaginable catastrophe.

These new sources of international instability are to some extent counteracted by the growing prestige of the United Nations Organization, which provides a valuable focus for international opinion, and a forum for the discussion of any disputes that arise. Though it has at present no overriding military power which could enforce peaceful settlements, and is gravely hampered by the veto, it can nevertheless mobilize formidable moral power which could influence the conduct of more moderate nations. It is, however, powerless against the actions of a ruthless aggressor, even if it almost unanimously opposes them, as the events in Hungary showed.

Nuclear weapons as a stabilizer

It is also likely that nuclear weapons have acted as a stabilizing force in international relations over the last decade. The consequences of a nuclear war are so serious that powerful nations are now prepared to accept unfavourable terms and grave humiliations rather than precipitate a war. A nuclear attack could not now be made on another nuclear power without bringing speedy and devastating retaliation, so that there would be no victors in a nuclear war, but only widespread death and destruction over the territories of the warring nations and over neighbouring countries as well. This has sunk deeply into the minds of modern statesmen, and has certainly restrained their instinctive reactions on several occasions. It is, however, less likely to influence unstable dictators jealous of their power and prestige.

The position is thus serious but not desperate. It is unlikely that a major conflict will break out in the near future, but there is a constant danger that one of the smaller conflicts that break out periodically will develop into a larger one. There is, however, a realization, even among nations addicted to expansion by brute force, that in future it would be less dangerous to expand by internal subversion. Thus even if they do not forgo their desire to extend their influence, it is to the advantage of the major powers to reduce and ultimately to eliminate the threat of nuclear war by the international control of nuclear weapons. It is along these lines of self-interest that practical progress is likely to be made.[1]

DISARMAMENT

Even without nuclear weapons, a war fought with the most modern conventional weapons would cause widespread suffering, as we know from the 1939–45 war. It is thus necessary to couple the control of nuclear weapons with a general disarmament embracing all offensive weapons, if a lasting peace is to be secured. This conclusion is reinforced by the problem of dealing with possible hidden stocks, which can only be effectively rendered useless by controlling conventional arms as well as nuclear weapons.

Though such a far-reaching disarmament programme may appear not only difficult to achieve, which it certainly is, but also thoroughly unrealistic, it is in fact the only way out of the present impasse which affords some hope of avoiding catastrophe. It has frequently happened in the past that neighbouring nations, once enemies, have learned to live with each other and are now amicable neighbours, separated by hundreds of miles of quite undefended frontier, between whom any recourse to arms has become quite unthinkable. A good example of this is in the history of the United States and Canada, but there are many others.

Co-existence

Even where there are deep differences of belief some form of peaceful co-existence can be evolved, like that now present

[1] Bacteriological warfare is beyond the scope of this book. See B. Chisholm, *BAS, 15,* 209 (1959); *BAS, 3,* 363 (1947); *BAS, 5,* 104 (1949); A. Haddow, "Bacteriological and Chemical Warfare", *NS, 5,* 329 (1959); *BAS, 15,* 337 (1959); *ASN, 1,* 90 (1947); "Symposium on Biological and Chemical Warfare", *BAS,* June 1960.

between Christian nations and Islam, once their most dangerous foe. Co-existence need not and should not imply indifference to the incompatibilities of belief. It is simply the recognition that they may be resolved over the years by charitable contacts and friendship, and that it is useless to precipitate a conflict that is highly likely to end in universal destruction.

There are two alternatives to controlled disarmament that are sometimes advocated and should be mentioned here. They are the two possible extremes, unilateral disarmament and preventive war.

Unilateral disarmament

Those in favour of the former course consider that nuclear weapons, or perhaps all weapons, are intrinsically evil and should be voluntarily and unilaterally relinquished by all nations. As the U.S.S.R. seem unlikely to do this we should set the good example and disarm ourselves. The U.S.S.R. may be impressed by the generous gesture and follow suit, or it may fill the power vacuum and gradually occupy the remainder of the world to suit its convenience. No student of international affairs is likely to have much doubt which of these alternatives would in fact happen. Furthermore, as has been seen in the chapter on the morality of nuclear warfare, a Government that disarmed unilaterally would be failing in its duty to provide for the defence of its people against possible aggression.

Preventive war

The opposite view is that the international crimes of the U.S.S.R. over the last decade have been so hideous that the Western nations, without waiting to be attacked, are justified in subjugating the U.S.S.R., thus liberating the enslaved nations and removing the threat to the peace of the world. Such a course of action might conceivably have been justified in other circumstances, when there was a good chance of it succeeding in its purpose without causing a disproportionate amount of harm. In existing circumstances, however, this is not the case. An attack of this kind would certainly plunge the world into its third, and probably last, great war. It has already been shown that there is no possibility of knocking out all the U.S.S.R. missile sites and aerodromes in a sudden, surprise blow. However vast and well-planned the initial strike, many sites and bombers would remain and would certainly be launched in a devastating counter-attack. In the ensuing conflict millions of casualties and unimaginable damage would be caused both to the great powers and to neutral and uncommitted nations as well. A preventive war would thus be an immoral act and an international crime of the greatest magnitude.

INTERNATIONAL CONTROL OF ATOMIC ENERGY

It remains therefore to consider the possibility of achieving a controlled general disarmament, and the steps most likely to prepare the way for it. It is instructive to recall some of the earliest efforts to achieve the international control of atomic energy, and then to consider the present situation in rather more detail.

The Lilienthal Report

The grave dangers of a world in which several powers possessed nuclear weapons was appreciated by scientists and politicians as soon as the first bombs were made, and early efforts were made to ensure that they could not be used again. In the United States, a Committee under the Chairmanship of Mr David E. Lilienthal and including among its members Dr J. R. Oppenheimer and Mr C. I. Barnard examined the whole problem of the international control of atomic energy.[2]

[2] *BAS, 1*, 8 (1946); *Symposium on the International Control of Atomic Energy*: Contributions from J. R. Oppenheimer, E. Teller, D. Inglis, E. Rabinowitch and others; *BAS, 1*, 12 (1946); *BAS, 2*, 1, 11 (1946); J. R. Oppenheimer, "Functions of the International Agency in Research and Development", *BAS, 3*, 173 (1947); D. E. Lilienthal, "Organization and Administration of the International Agency", *BAS, 3*, 203 (1947); "Operational and Developmental Functions of the International Agency", *BAS, 3*, 253 (1947).

They realized that since fissile material, once made, can be readily used either for peaceful purposes or for weapons the whole atomic energy industry, from the mining of the uranium ore to the final applications, has to be considered as a whole. Some parts of the industry are more sensitive than others. The mines, for example, need not be controlled closely because the uranium-bearing ore cannot be used directly. Likewise, the radioactive isotopes used for research or in other branches of industry cannot be used in weapons and so constitute no danger on that account.

The factories and power plants producing fissile material are the most critical parts of the industry, and require continuous and accurate control to prevent the diversion of any fissile material to clandestine purposes. This control would be technically feasible to apply, since these factories are so large that they could not be hidden. If this control were to fail, the fissile material could be made into weapons in a small factory that could easily escape detection. The results of these deliberations were embodied in the Lilienthal Report, which recommended the formation of an Atomic Development Authority and urged that energetic measures be taken to control atomic energy before it was too late.

The Baruch plan

The Lilienthal Report formed the basis of the Baruch plan, which was submitted by the United States to the Atomic Energy Commission of the United Nations General Assembly on June 14th, 1946.[3] The plan proposed the creation of an International Atomic Development Authority, which should be entrusted with all phases of the development and use of atomic energy from the raw materials to the final applications. All atomic energy activities potentially dangerous to world security would be owned by the Authority or subjected to effective managerial control, and it would be empowered to control, license and inspect all other atomic activities. It would have the duty of fostering the beneficial uses of atomic

[3] *BAS*, 2, 1 (1946).

energy, and of keeping in the forefront of the research and development on new ideas and techniques. When the Authority was established and the control system functioning, the plan went on to propose that no more bombs be manufactured, and existing bombs dismantled. Punishments were laid down for any violation of the rules of control, and the veto could not be used to protect any nation violating its solemn agreement not to develop or use atomic energy for destructive purposes. The United States offered to make all its accumulated experience and equipment available to the Authority. At that time, of course, only the United States had succeeded in making an atomic bomb.[4]

This plan was a bold, far-sighted and magnanimous gesture. Never before in history had a nation possessing a weapon of such power offered to relinquish it for the benefit of all nations. Had it been adopted many of the anxieties of the present time need not have arisen. Nevertheless, the plan had some serious disadvantages, especially when looked at through Russian eyes. They saw that it proposed the international ownership, or at least control, of all atomic energy activities. It was certain that a majority of the nations of the Council of the Authority would not be favourable to the U.S.S.R., and yet they would be able to decide the extent of atomic developments there. If they chose, they could, unhindered by the veto, obstruct or stifle the industrial progress of the whole country. This alone made the Baruch plan in its initial form unacceptable to the U.S.S.R.

However, the United States recognized when they submitted the plan that it might stand in need of modification, and expressed their willingness to enter into discussions with the aim of devising a plan that would be generally acceptable and yet adequate for its purpose. Unfortunately, instead of welcoming such discussions, the U.S.S.R. rejected the Baruch plan and submitted one of its own.[5]

[4] J. Hancock, "The U.S. Plan", *BAS*, *2*, 5 and 6, p. 14 (1946).
[5] "The American and Russian Proposals", *BAS*, *2*, 1 (1946).

The Soviet plan

The Soviet plan proposed that there should be an international agreement to prohibit the production and use of atomic weapons, to destroy existing stocks, and to condemn all activities undertaken in violation of the agreement. This act should be followed by the establishment of a system of control and by agreement on the sanctions to be applied against the unlawful use of atomic energy. The proposal to abolish the veto in atomic energy matters was rejected.

This plan was unacceptable to the West because it began with a purely verbal agreement to abolish nuclear warfare, and the practical steps to ensure this were relegated to a subsequent stage. A solemn agreement renouncing war as an instrument of national policy was already embodied in the United Nations Charter, and the pressing need was, and still is, for a way of effectively enforcing such an agreement. Since the nations do not trust each other, verbal agreements are valueless unless ways are devised to ensure that they are honoured. If the Soviet plan had been adopted the West would have had to disarm but would have had no way of being sure that the U.S.S.R. had done likewise. The West, reasonably enough, wanted the control body to be established and functioning before they disarmed.

Disarmament negotiations

Discussion of the two plans continued for a considerable time. The West continually pressed for the prior establishment of the control authority to ensure that the agreement to cease making nuclear weapons would be respected. The U.S.S.R. objected to some of the control proposals on the ground that they infringed national sovereignty, and appealed for an immediate agreement to ban the bomb.

While this discussion was continuing, the Scientific and Technical Committee of the United Nations was re-examining and extending the work of the Lilienthal Committee. They substantially agreed with its findings, and reported that: "We do not find any basis in the available scientific facts for supposing that effective control is not technologically feasible."[6]

This firmly returned the responsibility for reaching agreement to the statesmen, and during the subsequent years the United Nations Disarmament Sub-Committee held numerous meetings to try to reach agreement. Essentially, however, the deadlocks persisted, and although a number of elaborations and modifications were discussed, most of the time was spent in repeating and expounding the positions taken up during the discussions of the Baruch plan.[7]

Now, more than fifteen years after these discussions began, there is still no agreement. Many important developments have taken place, most of which have tended to make the problems of international control and disarmament even more difficult. In 1946 only the United States had nuclear weapons; in 1949 the U.S.S.R. exploded their first, and Great Britain and France followed in 1952 and 1960. It will not be long before they are joined by others. As soon as each nation developed an effective weapon they began to stockpile them as rapidly as the capacity of their production plants permitted.

It is now a much more complicated task to control nuclear weapons than it would have been in 1946. More nations would have to be subjected to control, with all their considerable atomic industries. Even so, it still remains technically feasible to control all existing factories and power plants producing fissile material, provided adequate funds are available

[6] "The Scientific and Technical Aspects of Atomic Energy Control", *BAS*, *2*, 7 and 8, 6 (1946); "First Report of the Atomic Energy Commission to the Security Council", *BAS*, *3*, 16 (1947).

[7] The Verbatim Reports of most of these discussions have been published by the United Nations Organization, but their sheer bulk makes them somewhat heavy reading. Convenient summaries have been published from time to time, e.g. K. Lonsdale, "A Chronology of the Negotiations for the International Control of Atomic Energy", *ASJ*, *4*, 67 (1954); P. J. Noel-Baker, *The Arms Race*, Stevens, 1958; R. W. Frase, "An Atomic Chronology", *The Nation*, June 18th, 1955, p. 559; A. Nutting, *Disarmament: An Outline of the Negotiations*. See also: J. R. Oppenheimer, "International Control of Atomic Energy", *BAS*, *4*, 39 (1948); Sir George Thomson, *ASN*, *2*, 77 (1949).

for a well-trained inspectorate to maintain continuous watch on all essential processes.

Hidden stocks of fissile material

The control of past production of fissile material is, however, a much more difficult problem. There is unfortunately no way of detecting, by any type of instrument, hidden stocks of fissile material. Furthermore, a retrospective estimate of past production, to determine how much should be handed over to the control authority is likely to be uncertain by at least ten per cent, and this represents a highly dangerous amount of fissile material. It would thus be easy for any of the nuclear powers to hide fissile material so that it could never be found by the control authority. The possible existence of such hidden stocks must therefore be accepted in any control plan, and steps taken to ensure that no nation would be able to make effective use of whatever stocks it may have concealed.

The control authority would have to keep in the van of weapons research so as to foresee and forestall new types of nuclear weapons.[8]

It is now generally accepted that any disarmament scheme will have to be put into practice by a series of stages of increasing difficulty. The first stage is the complete cessation of all tests of nuclear weapons. Then, when an effective control authority has been established, the manufacture and use of nuclear weapons may be prevented. Thirdly, all other offensive armaments will be brought under the control scheme.[9]

[8] A possible new weapon is a fission-free hydrogen bomb. This would be cheaper, more flexible and produce less radioactivity than existing bombs. See F. J. Dyson, "The Future Development of Nuclear Weapons", *Foreign Affairs*, April 1960, p. 457. D. R. Inglis, "Excessive Fear of Test Ban Evasion", *BAS, 16,* 168 (1960).

[9] An international group of scientists meets periodically to review the most practicable steps to take to avoid nuclear war. These are called Pugwash Conferences after the location of the first one. See *BAS, 13,* 243, 314 (1957); *14,* 118, 195, 338 (1958); *15,* 155, 376, 337 (1959); J. Rotblat, *NS, 4,* 1015 (1958).

DETECTION OF NUCLEAR EXPLOSIONS

Cessation of test explosions is chosen for the first stage mainly because it can be enforced without inspection teams entering any country, as is required by the subsequent stages. Most nuclear explosions can be detected by almost any nation that cares to set up the necessary equipment. It is therefore not necessary to trust the word of another country that it has stopped making test explosions; if it does make one it will not be able to conceal that it has broken the agreement. A subsidiary consideration is that cessation of tests prevents any further contamination of the atmosphere and retards development of new types of bombs. It is thus an attractive, clear-cut, intelligible and easily policed first stage in a series of disarmament negotiations.[10]

There has been some discussion about whether all nuclear tests can be detected at great distances. Most, if not all, of the tests made so far have been readily detected, but then no particular effort was made to hide them. Might it be possible for a nation, intent on evading the cessation agreement, to explode weapons in places, such as high in the stratosphere or deep in the earth, where the explosion might escape detection?

Airborne fission products

The detection of nuclear explosions depends on some physical effect being propagated from the explosion to an instrument able to record it. There are many such effects that can be used for long-distance detection.[11] The radioactive

[10] "Establishing International Control of Nuclear Explosions", *BAS* *14*, 262 (1958).

[11] J. C. Mark, "The Detection of Nuclear Explosions", *Nucleonics* (August), 64 (1959); "Tracing Nuclear Explosions", *BAS*, *9*, 44 (1953); J. Orear, "Detection of Nuclear Weapon Testing", *BAS, 14,* 98 (1958); E. K. Fedorov, "Controlled Cessation of Atomic Weapons Tests", *BAS, 15,* 8 (1959); H. Brown "Detection and Identification of Underground Nuclear Explosions", *BAS, 16,* 49, 89 (1960); T. Margerison, "Detection of Nuclear Bomb Tests", *NS, 4,* 1163 (1958); A. H. Rosenfeld, "Detection of Bomb Tests", Ch. 10 in *Fall-Out*, Ed. J. M. Fowler, Basic Books, New York, 1960.

fission products produced in the explosion are carried high into the stratosphere in the fireball and then dispersed over most of the earth's surface by the prevailing winds. This radioactive dust may be collected by aeroplanes and subjected to analysis. Less than a million-millionth of the debris, gathered in this way, can show that an explosion has taken place and can fix the approximate time it occurred. This method was used by the Americans and the British to detect the first Russian explosion in 1949. Samples of the upper air are now collected daily as a routine matter and examined for radioactivity, and there is a good chance of detecting a medium-sized explosion in this way. The method is useless, of course, if the explosion takes place underground, in ocean depths or high above the atmosphere. Most of the explosions that have taken place so far have been detected by this method.

Atmospheric waves

The powerful shock wave generated by the explosion affords another means of detection. This travels through the atmosphere and can be detected at great distances by sensitive microbarographs. Thus, for example, a typical signal due to a one-kiloton explosion at 1,000 km would be about 10 dynes per square cm. This method fails in the same conditions as the previous one, and is also liable to be rendered useless by high winds and other abnormal meteorological conditions.

Seismic waves

The shock wave also passes through the earth's crust, and is recorded on seismographs just like an earthquake. This is the best method of detecting underground explosions, but has the disadvantage that it could be confused with a natural earthquake, particularly if the explosion was deliberately timed to coincide with one. Muffling techniques have also been developed that can reduce the seismic effects of an underground explosion by as much as a factor of ten.[12] There are about five thousand earthquakes every year comparable in size to a five-kiloton explosion, so this possibility must be taken seriously. There are, however, a number of physical differences between the shock waves from explosions and earthquakes, and it may be possible to develop detecting techniques that will distinguish between them.

If the explosion takes place under water, a hydro-acoustic shock wave travels outwards and can readily be detected. Thus, a one-kiloton explosion would generate an excess pressure of about 35,000 dynes per square cm. at a distance of 1,000 km. It would, however, be difficult to decide who was responsible for such an explosion, and in any case it is unlikely that a test explosion would be made in mid-ocean due to the difficulty of recording its effects.

All the shock wave methods, in the air, on land and in the sea, can be used to fix the approximate site of the explosion, if the wave is recorded at three or more stations. As the wave then has different distances to travel, it will arrive at slightly different times and, knowing the velocity of the wave, its point of origin can be easily calculated.

Electromagnetic effects

Nuclear explosions also have electromagnetic effects that can be detected at a distance. These are not fully understood, but they are probably due to the current of Compton electrons produced by conversion of the gamma rays emitted from the fireball. The magnitude of the effect depends on the height of the explosion above the earth's surface, and typically a one-kiloton explosion can produce electric fields of about 10 millivolts per metre at distances of thousands of km. Heavy shielding around the source could reduce the effect to some extent, but as gamma rays are very penetrating this would not really be practicable. However, there are so many natural fluctuations of electric field intensity, or atmospherics,

[12] L. V. Berkner Report, June, 1959.

that this method is unreliable on its own. It could be used to confirm or rule out an explosion that had been indicated by another detection technique.

Some geomagnetic effects have also been recorded.[13] Their origin is complicated and it is not yet clear how useful they will be to detect explosions at large distances. If an explosion takes place at high altitudes, the electromagnetic effects disturb the ionosphere, and this can be recorded over a wide area.[14]

The flash of the explosion is visible at any place in the direct line of sight, provided the air is clear. Even for high-altitude explosions in the absence of cloud, however, a limit of about 500 miles is set by the curvature of the earth.

There are thus a considerable number of effects of nuclear explosions that can be detected at great distances, but most of them are liable to be masked for at least part of the time by natural fluctuations of the effect being measured. Several different methods used together are thus likely to give a far more reliable indication than any one on its own.

The explosions most difficult to detect are those at very high altitudes and those deep underground. It is rather unlikely that a clandestine test explosion would be made at high altitudes because of the difficulty of recording its effects and the danger that the rocket carrying it up would be detected by radar. Underground explosions are the easiest way to evade a test ban, for they can only be detected seismically.[15]

[13] S. Matsushita, "Geomagnetic and Ionospheric Phenomena associated with Nuclear Explosions", *Nature* (London), *184*, BA 33 (1959); J. A. Lawrie, V. B. Gerard, and P. J. Gill, "Magnetic Effects Resulting from Two High-Altitude Nuclear Explosions", *Nature* (London), *184*, BA 34 (1959); R. G. Mason and M. J. Vitousek, "Some Geomagnetic Phenomena associated with Nuclear Explosions", *Nature* (London), *184*, BA 52 (1959).

[14] C. H. Cummack and G. A. M. King, "Disturbance in the Ionospheric F-Region following the Johnston Island Nuclear Explosion", *Nature* (London), *184*, BA 32 (1959); S. Matsushita, *loc. cit.*

[15] "Bethe on Detection of Underground Explosions", *BAS, 15*, 257 (1959).

World-wide control

The detection system recently proposed in Geneva to ensure that no clandestine explosions take place therefore concentrated on establishing a network of control posts equipped with seismographs. It was estimated that about 160 land-based stations and ten ships would be sufficient to detect most explosions of more than one kiloton underground or in the atmosphere up to 10 km.[16] To distinguish explosions from earthquakes it is proposed that the stations be nearer together in regions of high seismic activity. Even then, about ten per cent of the earthquakes equivalent to a five-kiloton explosion and a large fraction of those equivalent to a one-kiloton explosion would be indistinguishable from nuclear explosions. There would thus always remain considerable difficulty in definitely identifying a concealed underground explosion.[17] It would always be possible, when necessary, to carry out a direct inspection in borderline cases.

The first stage of the proposed disarmament agreement is thus technically feasible, providing sufficient care was taken in the siting and construction of detecting stations. But even the relatively simple political problem of a controlled cessation of the nuclear tests has so far proved insoluble, and lengthy negotiations have taken place in Geneva without any definite result. The publicity given to the tests and the growing public opinion against them have, however, led to a voluntary cessation, but every power reserves the right to continue with their test programme if it should prove necessary. It seems unlikely that nations wanting to test their first bomb would be restrained for long by such a tacit agreement as this.

[16] "Experts' Conclusions on Test Detection", *BAS, 14*, 329 (1958); *BAS, 15*, 329 (1959); "Geneva Test Ban Negotiations: USSR, UK & US Reports", *BAS, 16*, 38 (1960).
[17] A. H. Rosenfeld, "What about the Undetectable Tests?" *BAS, 15*, 98 (1959); J. Orear, "How Feasible is a Test Ban?" *BAS, 15*, 99 (1959); H. H. Humphrey, "New Scientific Data and Test Ban Negotiations", *BAS, 15*, 109 (1959).

SUBSEQUENT STAGES

Deadlock having thus been reached in the first stage, it seems hardly realistic to spend much time on a detailed discussion of the subsequent stages, except to point out that they also are technically practicable within certain limits,[18] and that the most formidable obstacles are the political ones.

The second stage requires the establishment of an international inspectorate empowered to enter any industrial establishment in any country to make sure that no fissile material is being diverted from legitimate peaceful uses. With enough highly-trained inspectors it would be feasible to keep a sufficiently close watch on all nuclear reactors to ensure that this is substantially done. Nuclear power reactors, which produce the greatest amounts of fissile material, are so large that they would be impossible to conceal. The inspectorate would be fully equipped with the technical means of detection, including aerial photography and budgetary control. It might be more difficult to detect all the smaller research reactors, but these produce quite small amounts of fissile material. In any case, the possible or probable existence of stocks of fissile material concealed before the implementation of the agreement makes it hardly necessary for the inspection to be absolutely perfect.

The difficulty of achieving agreement to such inspection is so great that it seems almost inconceivable at the present time. No country would like to have such inspectors around, particularly those having much else to hide. There would also be the fear that legitimate trade secrets in industries quite unconnected with atomic energy would become known to the inspectors, and perhaps hence to their competitors. Never-

---

[18] S. Melman (Ed.), *Inspection for Disarmament*, Columbia University Press, 1958; S. Melman, "How can Inspection be made to Work?" *BAS, 14*, 270 (1958); L. Henkin, "Arms Inspection and the Constitution", *BAS, 15*, 192 (1959); P. J. Noel-Baker, *The Arms Race*, Stevens, 1958.

theless, the two major powers are already verbally committed to such an inspection scheme, and it is possible that over the years the political climate will change sufficiently to make its realization possible. There is certainly nothing to be lost by continually working towards such an agreement.

The probable existence of hidden stocks of nuclear weapons makes even the control of all industrial plants producing fissile material inadequate by itself to prevent a nuclear war. These hidden nuclear weapons could be rapidly brought into action, and delivered by the existing aeroplanes or by other means. The initial nuclear blow could be followed up by conventional forces.

For the reasons discussed already, there are so many ways of delivering nuclear weapons that it is impossible to prevent a surprise attack being launched. This is a very real danger that cannot be averted. It can, however, be reduced by ensuring, through a comprehensive disarmament embracing all the usual offensive weapons, especially aeroplanes, tanks and naval vessels, that it is impossible to follow up such a blow. The initial attack would then achieve nothing, and severe punishment would be imposed on the aggressor by the United Nations. There are few technical problems associated with the comprehensive disarmament of conventional weapons, since they must exist in large numbers to be effective, and this involves a vast amount of material that could not be concealed.

The United Nations Organization

An essential requirement for such a controlled disarmament is a strong and universally respected United Nations Organization, possessing armed forces of its own powerful enough to enforce the decisions taken, and able to punish, without hindrance from the veto, any attempt to evade the agreement.

If these efforts are successful, and the spectre of war gradually recedes, all the energies of scientists will become available for extending the frontiers of knowledge and applying their discoveries for the good of man.

Scientists form an international community that transcends national barriers. They think naturally in terms of a united world, and are constantly communicating with colleagues from overseas, and visiting them to attend conferences and study their work. This international cooperation is further strengthened by the complexity of modern research, especially in nuclear physics. Immense accelerating machines, too large for all but a few nations to build and use, are needed, with all their associated equipment and teams of operators. It is often best for them to be built as an international effort, as has happened for the 27-GeV proton synchrotron installed at CERN near Geneva.[19] This is an international laboratory supported by contributions from fourteen European nations and welcoming scientists from all over the world to come and work there.

There is no fear, if disarmament and international control are achieved, that scientists will be out of work. Many countries are desperately in need of skilled technical assistance, and suspension of war work will make available the resources to provide it. It will then be possible, without the cruel waste of war, to bring to all men the benefits of the advances in our understanding of the world that have come from the work of those who have laboured so long alone.

[19] T. G. Pickavance, "The European Nuclear Physics Laboratory", *ASJ, 3,* 73 (1953); Sir George Thomson, "European Centre for Nuclear Physics", *ASN, 1,* 123 (1952); L. Kowarski, "The Making of CERN", *BAS, 11,* 354 (1955); C. J. Bakker, "CERN as an Institute for International Co-operation", *BAS, 16,* 54 (1960); Sir Ben Lockspeiser, "Twelve Countries Combine in Nuclear Research", *NS, 12, 9* (1957).

SELECT BIBLIOGRAPHY

ASIMOV, I.: *Inside the Atom*, New York, Abelard-Schuman, 1956.

AUERBACH, C.: *Genetics in the Atomic Age*, New York, Essential Books, 1956.

BERTIN, L.: *Atom Harvest*, London, Secker and Warburg, 1957.

BORN, Max: *Atomic Physics*, London, Blackie, and New York, Hafner, 6th edn 1957.

COMPTON, A. H.: *Atomic Quest*, London and New York, Oxford Univ. Press, 1956.

CRAMMER, J. L., and PEIERLS, R. E. (Editors): *Atomic Energy*, Harmondsworth and Baltimore, Penguin Books, 1950.

DEAN, G.: *Report on the Atom*, London, Eyre and Spottiswoode, and New York, Knopf, 1954.

EPPSTEIN, J.: *Code of International Ethics*, London, Sands, 1953.

EVE, A. S.: *Rutherford*, Cambridge and New York, Cambridge Univ. Press, 1939.

FOWLER, J. M. (Editor): *Fallout*, New York, Basic Books, 1960.

HAWKINS, D. B. J.: *Man and Morals*, London and New York, Sheed and Ward, 1960.

HERSEY, J.: *Hiroshima*, Harmondsworth and Baltimore, Penguin Books, 1946.

JAY, K. E. B.: *Britain's Atomic Factories*, London, H.M. Stationery Office, 1954; *Calder Hall*, New York, Harcourt Brace, 1956.

JUNGK, R.: *Brighter than a Thousand Suns*, London, Gollancz, and New York, Hart-Davis, 1958.

KALMUS, H.: *Genetics*, Harmondsworth and Baltimore, Penguin Books, 1948.

LANSDELL, N.: *The Atom and the Energy Revolution*, Harmondsworth and Baltimore, Penguin Books, 1958.

LAPP, R. E.: *The Voyage of the Lucky Dragon*, Harmondsworth and Baltimore, Penguin Books, 1957.

LENIHAN, J. M. A.: *Atomic Energy and Its Applications*, London, Pitman, 1954.

MEDICAL RESEARCH COUNCIL: *The Hazards to Man of Nuclear and Allied Radiations*, London, H.M. Stationery Office, 1956.

MELMAN, S. (Editor): *Inspection for Disarmament*, New York, Columbia Univ. Press, 1958.

MICHIELS, J. L.: *Finding Out about Atomic Energy*, London, Watts, 1951.

NAGAI, T.: *We of Nagasaki*, London, Gollancz, and New York, Duell, 1951.

NOEL-BAKER, P. J.: *The Arms Race*, London, Stevens, 1958.

Oppenheimer, J. Robert, Transcript of Hearing before Personnel Security Board, Washington, U.S. Govt Printing Office, 1954.

Report of British Mission to Japan: *The Effects of the Atomic Bombs at Hiroshima and Nagasaki*, London, H.M. Stationery Office, 1946.

ROTBLAT, J. (Editor): *Atomic Energy, A Survey*, London, Taylor and Francis, 1954.

SCHUBERT, J., and LAPP, R. E.: *Radiation: What it is and How it Affects You*, London, Heinemann, and New York, Viking Press, 1957.

SMYTH, H. D.: *A General Account of the Development of the Methods of Using Atomic Energy for Military Purposes under the United States Government*, London, H.M. Stationery Office, and Washington, U.S. Govt Printing Office, 1945.

SHTERNFELD, A.: *Soviet Space Science*, New York, Basic Books, 1959.

SNOW, C. P.: *The New Men*, Harmondsworth and Baltimore, Penguin Books, 1959; *The Two Cultures and the Scientific Revolution*, Cambridge and New York, Cambridge Univ. Press, 1959.

STRANATHAN, J. D.: *The Particles of Modern Physics*, Philadelphia, Blakiston, 1946.

THOMSON, J. J.: *Recollections and Reflections*, London, Bell, 1936.

VAN MELSEN, A. G.: *From Atomos to Atom*, Pittsburgh, Pa, Duquesne Univ. Press, 1952.

The Twentieth Century Encyclopedia of Catholicism

The number of each volume indicates its place in the over-all series and not the order of publication.

All titles are subject to change.